Oath of Ahimsa

*Before I begin, I want to make it unequivocally clear that **my support for political activism in the interests of defending Dharma is strictly in terms of non-violence**. This is about challenging bad beliefs and ideas. Most Hindus, Buddhists, Jains, Sikhs, and related followers of Sanatana Dharma would agree and believe this Oath to be unnecessary and obvious. Some may even nitpick this oath on the nuances of Ahimsa's meaning regarding cases of self-defense. **Nevertheless, the core of Ahimsa is non-violence and if you're going to be using this work that I've compiled, then I want you to make an oath of non-violence to yourself right now on my behalf. My interests in writing this as a self-identified Hindu Atheist are in criticizing what I find to be the harmful ideas of Christianity that Christians hold. I will never condone any violence or discrimination against Christian people. This is about criticizing Christianity, it is not about bigotry and violence towards Christians.** Criticizing Jesus Christ's claim to godhood is not support for banning Christian religious festivals or threatening violence against Christians. Christian missionaries are annoying and they have ridiculous beliefs, but my interests are in criticizing those annoying and ridiculous beliefs. They are never and will never be in hurting Christian people, missionaries or otherwise. **You may only use this work if you agree with an oath of non-violence against Christians.** Christians are simply fallible human beings filled with bigoted and generally narcissistic beliefs, but*

1

that doesn't nor shall it ever justify any violence. If you cannot make this pledge for me to yourself and keep it, then there is nothing for you here and you should stop reading. If, however, you think this was unnecessary and you'll obviously never support violence against Christians, then please continue reading.

Table of Contents

Chapter 1: Effectively Communicating the Falseness of Christianity . . . Pages 6 – 27

Chapter 2: Exposing Christianity: Use the Bible to disprove the Bible . . . Pages 28 – 114

- *How about where Yahweh of the Bible condones and commands murder and genocide? (Genesis 7:18–23, Exodus 12:29, Exodus 32:27–29, Deuteronomy 13:6-11, Numbers 31:17)* Pgs. 32 – 41
- *Or maybe blood sacrifice of animals, children, and his own "son?" (Exodus 20:24, Hebrews 9:22, Leviticus 1:9, Judges 11:30–39, Hebrews 10:10)* Pgs. 42 – 54
- *Gratuitous torture? (Revelation 9:5-6, Revelation 20:10-15)* Pgs. 55 – 58
- *Murder and abuse of children? (2 Samuel 12:15-18, 2 Kings 2:23-24)* Pgs. 59 – 64
- *Cruel indifference towards animal suffering? (Joshua 11:6, Genesis 7:18-23)* Pgs. 65 – 68
- *Theft and destruction? (Deuteronomy 20:13-14, Luke 19:30-35)* Pgs. 69 – 75
- *How about slavery? (Leviticus 25:44-46, Exodus 21:7, 1Peter 2:18, Exodus 21:20-21)* Pgs. 76 – 77
- *How about pedophilia, incest, and rape? (Genesis 3:20, Genesis 19:8 and 19:36, Judges 19: 23-29, Numbers 31:17-18, 2 Peter 2:7-8(in reference to Lot offering his daughters in Genesis 19:8), Deuteronomy 22:28-29(a raped virgin must marry her rapist)* Pgs. 78 – 91
- *Threatening that if people disobey him or worship other gods, he will force them to eat their own children? (Jeremiah 19:9, Leviticus 26:27-29)* Pgs. 92 – 98

3

- *Betrayal? (Hebrews 10:9-10, Exodus 10:1, 1Peter 5:8[where the Bible god betrays all of humanity by allowing Satan to roam about the earth])* **Pgs 99 – 101**
- *Lying, and making other people lie? (Genesis 22:2, Genesis 8:21, 2Peter 3:10-11[contradicting god's promise in Gen. 8:21, to never again destroy the Earth], Ezekiel 14:9[Where god deliberately deceives a prophet], 1Kings 22:23, 2Thessalonians 2:11)* **Pgs. 102 – 103**
- *The New Testament and Jesus Christ's teachings of Hatred towards family, Hatred of Jews, and Oppression and Hatred of women* **Pgs. 104 – 122**

Chapter 4: My Opinion on Evangelical Christianity and How to Prevent its Growth . . . Pages 123 – 140

Chapter 5: Examples of Questions to Ask Christian Missionaries . . . Pages 141 – 179

- Section 1: Original Sin . . . Pgs. 145 – 148
- Section 2: Christian Heaven Pgs. 149 – 151
- Section 3: Christian Rape crimes, the Holocaust, and The United States wars Pgs. 152 – 163
- Section 4: Transgender People and God . . . Pgs. 164 – 176
- Section 5: The end of the world Pgs. 177 – 179

Chapter 6: Resources . . . Pages 180 – 239

Bibliography . . . Pages 240 – 241

About the Author . . . Page 242

Copyright Notice . . . Page 242

Chapter 1: Effectively Communicating the Falseness of Christianity

Forced conversions have gained increasing attention in India's national media and likewise forced conversions has been an issue patently ignored by the majority of the Western news media or otherwise falsely re-contextualized as Hindus being bigoted towards Christians when the truth is the opposite in most encounters. What many Western journalists refuse to acknowledge is the chronic narcissism of Christian missionaries due to the teachings of Christianity professing that Christians are all chosen people and their unabashed hatred of non-Christian cultures and civilizations. I've been personally concerned by what manipulative tactics these Christian missionaries could be using, which was why I wrote a book to help Indians stop forced conversions in India. My belief was that highlighting the moral and logical flaws of Christianity at their source would help to stifle or overturn any trend of conversion tactics. I don't know how effective my help has been, but it has been my intention to defend Dharmic faiths and culture while dismantling

Christian missionary efforts. I hope any contributions I make can help in that effort, but I'm worried that my previous book didn't do enough for that intended purpose. My intent is to destroy Christianity at its source by de-legitimizing it in the views of its followers. I've become increasingly concerned with the social media response whereby Hindus throughout social media seem to be falling prey to Christian conversion tactics by fearmongering Christian conversions, pursuing political agendas that try to ban conversions outright without the distinction that they should be trying to ban only forced conversions which is a nefarious and deliberately manipulative tactic of using financial influence to demand changing one's faith, and I've seen blog posts by Hindus denouncing Christian conversions as having successfully harmed family units within India. Unfortunately for many Hindus who want to put a stop to conversion tactics, all this does is serve as confirmation to Christian missionaries that their tactics are working. Moreover, Christian missionaries perceive this response by Hindus to mean that Hinduism is losing to the so-called "truth" of Jesus Christ's message and it only emboldens them further to continue to pursue and increase Christian missionary activities. They believe the fear of Hindus towards mass conversions is proof of Christianity, because their holy book teaches them that people who deny Christianity are afraid because any people denying Jesus Christ's message somehow "know" that it is true and that's why they're denying it. The Monotheistic faiths are filled with these bizarre forms of narcissistic circular reasoning which their followers are taught to ignore the logical inconsistencies of. Nevertheless, if you're a follower of the Dharmic faiths and you care about preserving Dharmic culture and civilization, then you should be trying to expose the falseness of Christianity. Don't simply shy away and cry about fears of mass conversions, directly confront these Christian missionaries by spreading doubt in their minds and exposing their unyielding faith to horrifying doubts that shake their trust in Jesus Christ; in other words, *put their faith in doubt.*

It is my hope that I can help fellow followers of Dharma to put the shining unquestioned faith of Christian missionaries into complete despair, confusion, and to give them a constant exposure of questioning that causes crises upon crises of faith for Christian missionaries. Not just to defend Hinduism and all Dharmic faiths more generally, but to change the perception of Christian missionaries towards India as not an inferior country to Western ones that exists to harvest billions of souls for Jesus, but as a place that they go warily to test the faith of their most faithful flock because they're exposed to so many hard questions that prove how brittle and false Christianity truly is. India should become similar to Japan in this regard whereby the country is not seen as ripe for harvest for hopeful missionaries, but as one of dread and painful disappointment that missionaries try to downplay the relevance of because the abysmal failure means their dreams of Christianity taking over the world has come to a grinding halt; their attempts at affirming their own faith through conversions has instead resulted in stirring more doubts within them. To that end, Dharmic followers cannot respond to criticism online with vague and pro-isolationist responses such as "You don't know what's happening in India because you don't live here!" as that quite honestly just makes other people think that Dharmic followers are hiding bad deeds and it convinces neutral observers that people accusing Dharmic followers of nefarious behavior are speaking truthfully. It is much more effective for the Dharmic cause by highlighting facts that you do know that are happening or have happened in India and sharing them with people online who wrongfully accuse Hindus and other Dharmic followers of misdeeds. Sharing facts that are generally unknown to people who trust the Western news media would be far more effective in giving people pause and causing them to question what they think they know about India. For example, sharing news about the still active Christian terrorist organization called the National Liberation Front of Tripura, which was created by New Zealand Baptist Churches, and spread violent terrorism upon Hindus by Baptist Christian converts who turned to terrorism to spread the Christian faith and to carve a small Christian nation-state out of the body of India.[1] This would go a long way in causing many people,

---

[1] "National Liberation Front of Tripura." Wikipedia, Wikimedia Foundation, 9 Nov. 2020, en.wikipedia.org/wiki/National_Liberation_Front_of_Tripura.

especially Christians in the West who are unaware of these facts, to

distrust Christian institutions, to potentially distrust their own

donations to Christian organizations, and break any uniformity of

opinion that non-Christians may have with Christians on issues that

involve India. After all, this is a Christian terrorist organization that

was initially funded by a Western country for the explicit purpose of

killing Indians; the majority of people of any country do not want to

harm innocent people or support any form of terrorism and

emphasizing terrorist organizations with religious roots and religious

objectives will cause doubt among followers of that faith, especially

if they had no knowledge of these terrorist organizations prior to you

sharing credible information about them. It has a domino effect and

does far greater damage to the cause of Christian conversions than

simply arguing foreign people don't understand India. You create

change by exposing the truth and sharing what you know. Don't just

be a reactionary spectator howling about how nobody has any right

to an opinion on India except people who live in India, because

that'll never work and it is the tactic of brutal and repressive regimes like China. Use the knowledge you have on terrorist organizations like NLFT[2], scandals such as pedophile crimes by Catholic priests in India[34], and other such information that is usually referencing truthful personal accounts to make people doubt what they think they know; don't just argue they don't understand India, *show proof of why they don't understand India's national issues.* Don't just try to dismiss and shut down conversations, but rather communicate effectively.

A problematic development that I've noticed is that many Hindus from India seem to have adapted and are using Abrahamic terminology when describing Hinduism. In particular, the phrases "idol worship" and "paganism" and similar terms are historically

[2] "SOUTH ASIA | 'Church Backing Tripura Rebels'." BBC News, BBC, 18 Apr. 2000, news.bbc.co.uk/2/hi/world/south_asia/717775.stm.

[3] Sudhakaran, P. "Former Nun's Autobiography to Expose Catholic Church's Crisis in Kerala: Thiruvananthapuram News - Times of India." The Times of India, TOI, timesofindia.indiatimes.com/city/thiruvananthapuram/Former-Nuns-autobiography-to-expose-Catholic-Churchs-crisis-in-Kerala/articleshow/12476427.cms.

[4] Dutt, Barkha. "Opinion | In India, a Nun's #MeToo Moment Exposes the Failings of the Catholic Church." The Washington Post, WP Company, 1 Apr. 2019, www.washingtonpost.com/news/global-opinions/wp/2018/09/14/in-india-a-nuns-metoo-moment-exposes-the-failings-of-the-catholic-church/?utm_term=.6480250609be.

rooted in bigotry against non-Abrahamic faiths as a way of implying

that they're somehow defective because they're not monotheistic.

This sort of language must be overturned, because it is unfair and

frankly nonsensical to claim that being a monotheist is somehow

more rational than being any other type of theist. None of these

supernatural beliefs have any evidence of being true, so it is

completely wrong to label any of them as more false or somehow

dumber than others. To be clear, being a monotheist isn't more likely

to be true than being a polytheist because in terms of statistical

evidence and pure rational logic, you need to prove that an element

or variable actually exists and has made a falsifiable occurrence in

the world. Thus, Hindus are *not* defective for being polytheistic,

monistic, pantheistic, henotheistic, atheistic, or whatever else when

compared to any monotheist. If you have ever felt that as a Hindu

and felt the need to re-contextualize Hindu theology into more

monotheistic terms similar to the Abrahamic faiths, then please be

rest assured that you are not lesser for believing in multiple deities,

any other variation of deities, or even no deity. Being an "idol worshipper" or a "Pagan" doesn't make you lesser than any monotheist and it doesn't mean that your beliefs are dumber or more defective than any form of monotheism. I felt it was important to explicitly make this clear, because it honestly seems as if Hindus have internalized this idea that polytheistic viewpoints are somehow defective compared to monotheistic ones.

To change the implicit anti-Dharmic bias of the terminology, it is imperative to change the language that we use when discussing different religions with fellow Hindus, fellow Dharmic followers, and especially with Christian missionaries. I had previously encouraged fellow Dharmic followers to challenge anti-Speech laws in India in defense of Dharmic beliefs, but I realize too late that I was unfairly asking too much of people. There's surely a better way of exposing Christianity's falsehoods. What is important to communicate effectively is referring to Christianity's falseness while maintaining respect for other religions in accordance with India's laws and respect for the general community. For that purpose, consider referring to Christianity with statements such as "The mythology of Christianity", "Biblical mythology", "The myth of Jesus", "The mythological story of Jesus Christ", "The myth of the Exodus", or "Christian mythology" when talking to Christian missionaries or fellow Dharmic followers. In this manner, we implicitly communicate that Christianity is false and that we don't consider its claims to be truth without personally insulting Christians or Christian missionaries. If, for instance, they try to accuse you of insulting their faith, you can easily make the defense that calling it Christian mythology is just your personal belief because you honestly don't believe in it. Try to come-up with techniques or phrases that effectively communicate Christianity as mythology to Christian missionaries because it directly communicates to them that Christianity is false without getting into legal troubles for speaking your mind. If they respond by calling Hinduism mythology, then that is fine because we've now equaled the playing field and they're not using narcissistic terms like idol worship and paganism to ridicule Hindus as inferior to them. However, if they deride Hinduism as idol worship or paganism more furiously, then they're openly displaying hostility and contempt for Hindus which others can plainly see and you can accuse them of being insecure in their Christian beliefs which is why they're using such derogatory language towards other religions. You can accuse them of being filled with hate and that all they're showing is that Christianity preaches hatred for others which is why they're using such insults. If you wish to de-escalate potentially hostile encounters, explain that you're just "being curious about Christianity" which is why you're talking to them or otherwise use your best judgment in explaining how Christian missionaries ask potential converts "to be curious about Christianity" but you find that they're being very rude and not answering your questions whenever they act hostile to you.

If you don't think these communication tactics will work or wish for a more direct criticism of Christianity, then consider accusing Christian missionaries of believing in a self-denying polytheistic faith that doesn't understand basic math. All monotheistic faiths are self-denying polytheistic faiths because they don't just believe in One God as they claim, but believe in an innumerable amount of angels who behave as "Messengers" with no freewill.[5] These angels in the Abrahamic faiths with their many bizarre classifications and rankings from Archangels, guardian angels, winged angels, and others are treated as equivalent to Hindu Devas and Devis by some Western religious scholars; some Western religious scholars, who seem intent on trying to passively label Hinduism as inferior, have taught the misconception that some Devas and Devis are "demigods" and therefore equivalent to the Abrahamic concept of angels. While I disagree with this, since Hindu theology teaches personal Gods are but different forms of the unity of Brahman and is open enough to include atheism as part of its Truthseeking, this nonsensical argument by Western religious scholars opens up criticism of the Abrahamic faiths being polytheistic since they're comparing angels to what they perceive to be lesser Gods. Of course, Westerners make a special exception for Jesus Christ and don't consider him a Demigod despite him fitting the definition due to having the Abrahamic God as a Father and the

---

[5] "How Many Angels Are There?" GotQuestions.org, 13 May 2019, www.gotquestions.org/how-many-angels-are-there.html.

Virgin Mary as a mother. Even without this unintended suggestion by the ignorance of some Western religious scholars, the very behavior and purpose of the concept of angels does open-up an argument that all the Abrahamic faiths are just self-denying polytheistic faiths because the angels have no freewill and serve only the purpose of the Abrahamic God, Yahweh (or Jehovah in some translations of the name) in Abrahamic theology. Use the research provided at the end of this book and try to formulate your own arguments to criticize Christian missionaries on the basis that they follow a self-denying polytheism. The following chapters will contain resources that you can read at your own time and use to devise your own strategies and questions for the purpose of confronting Christian missionaries with the reality that their religion is heavily stolen from the very paganism that they hate. Christianity's trinity is stolen from the very "pagan" mythologies like Celtic mythology's Goddess Morrigan who is known for her triple Goddess form of Maiden, Mother, and Crone which Christianity copied to create Father, Son, and Holy Spirit.[6] The Bible contains no mention of a Holy Trinity, but Christians attempt to "reinterpret" the Bible to suit their conveniences. Confront Christian missionaries about the self-contradiction in their own theology about using a historically rooted pagan belief in a triple deity while claiming to be monotheistic. The story of Jesus Christ's descent to hell and rise to heaven is stolen from the story of Inanna the Sumerian Goddess known as Queen of Heaven in Sumerian mythology.[7][8] Devise you own questions to confront Christian missionaries about the Jesus story being completely stolen from the Inanna and Dumuzi story which was written in cuneiform in 2100 BCE in what is now modern-day Iraq far before the Bible was ever written.[9] Be direct, precise, and to the point in your conversations with them to make them begin doubting their faith in Biblical mythology. Be clear in communicating that you don't believe in Christianity because it is

[6] "Triple Deity." Wikipedia, Wikimedia Foundation, 29 Oct. 2020, en.wikipedia.org/wiki/Triple_deity.
[7] Ishtar's Descent into the Underworld (Page 1), www.inanna.virtualave.net/tammuz.html.
[8] Tarico, Valerie. "Ancient Sumerian Origins of the Easter Story." HuffPost, HuffPost, 25 May 2011, www.huffpost.com/entry/ancient-mythic-origins-of_b_185455.
[9] Tarico, Valerie. "Ancient Sumerian Origins of the Easter Story." HuffPost, HuffPost, 25 May 2011, www.huffpost.com/entry/ancient-mythic-origins-of_b_185455.

mythology and formulate criticisms expressing why Christianity is false.

In the following chapters, I'll add specific texts from the Bible that challenge Christianity on moral grounds and the final chapter will have cited resources. The resources chapter will have my own commentary from my previous book, Faith in Doubt, because it pertains to the lack of archaeological evidence for the Bible. For this chapter, I'll end with the question that seems to cause the most difficulty for Christians to answer and it is probably the most useful question insofar as I could formulate. I asked a Christian subreddit under the guise of another username, and they were dumbstruck by the question. For greater context, this specific event in the Bible supposedly happened when Jesus was resurrected and is presumably proof of his resurrection. I searched for what Christian Ministers and Pastors say happened to these specifically listed people, and most of what I've found is that these people who presumably also resurrected were said to have gone home and died natural deaths with no explanation. Every time I ask Christians this question, it is completely avoided. I could say it in the nicest way possible and they don't respond. Doesn't matter what kind of Christian: Fundamentalist, Orthodox, Baptists, Liberal denominations, etc. Nobody answers the questions I have about these verses. With that said here it is:

If the Bible is truly the Word of God and Jesus Christ really did resurrect, then why is there no record of the people mentioned in Matthew 27:52-53 who apparently came back from the dead the same time Jesus Christ did?

Matthew 27:52-53 King James Version

52 And the graves were opened; and many bodies of the saints which slept arose,

53 And came out of the graves after his resurrection, and went into the holy city, and appeared unto many.

Why didn't these Saints, who according to the Bible walked out of their graves, write their own testimonials into the Bible itself to prove Jesus was God? Why is there no record or evidence of these people returning from the dead outside of the Bible? Why is there no history of what they did after resurrecting the same time as Jesus, if they really came back?

One website answered the question with a feeble: "they went back home and died natural deaths again"[10] and an apologist Christian Minister who claims it is true because priests were willing to die for it claims the other resurrections aren't true but Jesus's is somehow true.[11] Of course, dying for your religious faith doesn't prove that it is true because truth is based on empirical evidence. It is insane to think that dying for a belief raises the value of its truth. For example, arguments that "dying for the faith means it is true" could promote and justify suicide bombers. Regardless, there is no evidence that these Abrahamic saints resurrected or even existed and this lie about a resurrection happened at the exact time that Jesus Christ himself is said to have resurrected. This is very damaging to Christianity's claim of being revealed truth because the resurrection was supposed to be proof that Jesus was the Son of God according to modern Christianity, and yet there are claims of these saints

[10] "What Happened to the Resurrected Saints Mentioned in Matthew 27: 52-53?" United Church of God, 9 Nov. 2010, www.ucg.org/bible-study-tools/bible-questions-and-answers/what-happened-to-the-resurrected-saints-mentioned-in.
[11] Licona, Mike. Were People Raised When Jesus Died? Youtube, 28 Apr. 2020, www.youtube.com/watch?v=rn50_pjn5Cg&feature=youtu.be.

resurrecting after him and these saints are presumably not the direct Son of God as Jesus Christ is claimed to be. Modern Christians have mostly never heard of that portion of the story, but those who have either admit that all these other resurrection claims are false while giving special pleading arguments that Jesus Christ's story is somehow true or they throw all rational logic out the window to claim the resurrections of saints also happened despite lack of evidence, lack of testimonials from these supposed saints, the fact these supposed people didn't write any holy books of their own which could have helped to give more credibility to Jesus's self-proclaimed godhood, and the lack of any historical evidence on their lives after supposedly resurrecting from death.

It must be made clear that the quickest and most effective way of disproving the Bible is to share knowledge on the facts pertaining to its authenticity. The claim by Christians and Christian missionaries that the Bible is the most historically accurate book is entirely false. Israeli Archaeology had to regretfully tell the world that after thirty-five years of digging on the ancient sites of supposed

Biblical events that the vast majority of the contents of the Bible are complete mythology.[12] Many of these archaeologists were Jews and Christians who felt deeply connected to the fantasy stories of the Bible itself and had to painfully come to terms with the understanding that there was no evidence to support what was deeply precious beliefs to them. They bravely told the whole world the honest truth of the matter due to their commitments to academic integrity and truth. We should applaud these brave researchers for their integrity and strength of character to tell the whole world that there is no evidence to support many of the Bible's claims. The most important and shocking revelation was that there was no evidence to support the story of Exodus; the Israelites were never slaves to Egypt, there was never a plague that killed the firstborn in Egypt, Egypt has no record of Israelites as slaves, a group of two million Israelites never wandered the desert for forty years and there is not a shred of evidence to support that such an event ever happened, ancient Israelites were polytheists and only gradually became

---

[12] "Archeology of the Hebrew Bible." PBS, Public Broadcasting Service, 18 Nov. 2008, www.pbs.org/wgbh/nova/ancient/archeology-hebrew-bible.html.

monotheist over the centuries usually due to famine, for a lengthy period of Israelite history the god Yahweh had a Goddess wife named Asherah, and there is no evidence to support that the person known as Prophet Moses ever existed.[13] The claims by Christian extremists that Egypt must have destroyed all evidence is both fatuous and an argument that essentially states they believe that Exodus and the Bible are true *because* there is no evidence for it; the thinly veiled nonsense is easy to see-through. *They believe it is true, because they have no evidence for it.* They are not ready to face the reality about their sacred beliefs and will probably deny it with either lies or try to suggest some Christian apologist Youtuber who has no academic credibility compared to actual archaeologists who spent 35 years researching and excavating the sites of the ancient Israelites. All that said, I strongly recommend reading everything in the resource section to form a greater understanding of this issue and to use this research of the archaeological findings to form your questions in order to effectively challenge Christian missionaries on

[13] "Archeology of the Hebrew Bible." PBS, Public Broadcasting Service, 18 Nov. 2008, www.pbs.org/wgbh/nova/ancient/archeology-hebrew-bible.html.

the authenticity of their Christian beliefs and the Bible itself. I understand people can be pressed for time, but I'd strongly recommend making copies and sharing both these news articles with Hindus who think the Jewish Prophet Moses was a real person. I've added website links for information that was too large to put in a single, physical book or which linked to videos. I recommend using those sources too, if you believe it'll help in criticizing Christian missionaries and formulating your own questions against Christianity.

I hope this has been a valuable and insightful resource. Please let me know in emails to jovejarin@hotmail.com whether this has helped or please provide constructive comments on how to improve. I don't find this "*You don't understand Sanatana Dharma!*" rebuke helpful in effectively addressing Dharmic grievances in either political interests for equality or human rights more generally. We need to start effectively communicating with both fellow Dharmic followers and non-Dharmic followers if we want political goals to be met.

Chapter 2: Exposing Christianity: Use the Bible to disprove the Bible

For the purposes of honesty and integrity, I felt that it was necessary that you can read the full quote and determine for yourselves if you believe that it is taken out of context. For the purposes of ease of access, I've decided to bold the specific portions of the Biblical verses that are disturbing to balance understanding the context with getting to the point. The only ones not fully quoted are what I found to be less important verses such as the section on lying since that's a ubiquitous issue among all societies and isn't as horrifying as the Bible's encouragement for incest, rape, murder, and misogyny. If you think I've mischaracterized them, then please feel free to read the full quotes as they should be freely available online. These are all from the King James version which I am using because it is in the public domain of copyright law. The chief purpose of this method is to *use the Bible to refute the Bible* when opposing Christian missionary conversions and to assist those who oppose conversion practices with knowledge in order to stymie or fully overturn Christian conversion practices by making them useless. If people are exposed to the knowledge of Christianity's falsehoods, will they convert if they wish to maintain an honest life?

A criticism that'll perhaps be pointed out by Christian apologists is that I'm quoting the Old Testament in much of this. Indeed, a lot of this is the Old Testament and while modern-day Christians (even missionaries) may say that the Old Testament isn't relevant, please keep in mind that they're literally saying that you should believe in the morals of their holy book by ignoring half of it which is no longer of value. Their argument that it is no longer relevant is usually for some vague reason pertaining to Moses's Law, often referred to as the Mosiac Law, either being fulfilled or destroyed by Jesus Christ. Depending on the Christian denomination, the particulars of Jesus destroying or fulfilling the Mosiac law and what that even means differs depending upon the multitude of Christian denominations who can't even agree on basic terms of what this concept is and argue the "other Christian denominations" are simply speaking falsely. Confused? The truth is, so are Christians themselves, so they ignore this by trying to emphasize it is somehow true despite either confusing Christian history for their own personal interpretations or trying to change the subject to the supposed "peaceful" or "truthful" teachings of Jesus Christ. However, the fact remains that the Exodus story lacks any archaeological evidence of being true and has thus been debunked as a fictional story for more than forty years now. That means there is no evidence to support that Moses existed and if Moses didn't exist, then how could Jesus Christ's claim of fulfilling or destroying the Mosiac Law as a claim to his godhood be true?

I had hoped to add several independent questions similar to that for each of these sections, but the sheer breadth of the resources made that somewhat impossible. I've opted to share example questions in Chapter 5 to help people formulate their own questions. I'll just have to trust in people to form their own effective arguments. The following are broken-up into sections; I learned of these disturbing passages thanks to communication on a religious debate forum on Facebook and decided to make use of them. I hope this post has been useful to peaceful pro-Dharmic social causes opposing Christian conversions. The main point is to use the Bible to disprove the Bible, so that Christian conversion is effectively made impossible and to spread doubt on the authenticity of Christianity for Christian missionaries themselves so that they're less likely to continue missionary activities. Combine your use of this section with the links to archaeological research in the previous section to help form your arguments to scrutinize and spread doubt about the Christian faith.

Genesis 7: 14-24 KJV

14 They, and every beast after his kind, and all the cattle after their kind, and every creeping thing that creepeth upon the earth after his kind, and every fowl after his kind, every bird of every sort.

15 And they went in unto Noah into the ark, two and two of all flesh, wherein is the breath of life.

16 And they that went in, went in male and female of all flesh, as God had commanded him: and the LORD shut him in.

17 And the flood was forty days upon the earth; and the waters increased, and bare up the ark, and it was lift up above the earth.

18 And the waters prevailed, and were increased greatly upon the earth; and the ark went upon the face of the waters.

19 And the waters prevailed exceedingly upon the earth; and all the high hills, that were under the whole heaven, were covered.

20 Fifteen cubits upward did the waters prevail; and the mountains were covered.

21 And all flesh died that moved upon the earth, both of fowl, and of cattle, and of beast, and of every creeping thing that creepeth upon the earth, and every man*:*

22 All in whose nostrils was the breath of life, of all that was in the dry land, died*.*

*23 And every living substance was destroyed which was upon the face of the ground, **both man**, and cattle, and the creeping things, and the fowl of the heaven; and **they were destroyed from the earth**: and Noah only remained alive, and they that were with him in the ark.*

24 And the waters prevailed upon the earth an hundred and fifty days.

&

Exodus 12: 12-30 KJV

12 For I will pass through the land of Egypt this night, and will smite all the firstborn in the land of Egypt, both man and beast; and against all the gods of Egypt I will execute judgment: I am the Lord.

13 And the blood shall be to you for a token upon the houses where ye are: and when I see the blood, I will pass over you, and the plague shall not be upon you to destroy you, when I smite the land of Egypt.

14 And this day shall be unto you for a memorial; and ye shall keep it a feast to the Lord throughout your generations; ye shall keep it a feast by an ordinance for ever.

15 Seven days shall ye eat unleavened bread; even the first day ye shall put away leaven out of your houses: for whosoever eateth leavened bread from the first day until the seventh day, that soul shall be cut off from Israel.

16 And in the first day there shall be an holy convocation, and in the seventh day there shall be an holy convocation to you; no manner of work shall be done in them, save that which every man must eat, that only may be done of you.

17 And ye shall observe the feast of unleavened bread; for in this selfsame day have I brought your armies out of the land of Egypt: therefore shall ye observe this day in your generations by an ordinance for ever.

18 In the first month, on the fourteenth day of the month at even, ye shall eat unleavened bread, until the one and twentieth day of the month at even.

19 Seven days shall there be no leaven found in your houses: for whosoever eateth that which is leavened, even that soul shall be cut off from the congregation of Israel, whether he be a stranger, or born in the land.

20 Ye shall eat nothing leavened; in all your habitations shall ye eat unleavened bread.

21 Then Moses called for all the elders of Israel, and said unto them, Draw out and take you a lamb according to your families, and kill the passover.

22 And ye shall take a bunch of hyssop, and dip it in the blood that is in the bason, and strike the lintel and the two side posts with the blood that is in the bason; and none of you shall go out at the door of his house until the morning.

*23 **For the Lord will pass through to smite the Egyptians**; and when he seeth the blood upon the lintel, and on the two side posts, the Lord will pass over the door, and will not suffer the destroyer to come in unto your houses to smite you.*

24 And ye shall observe this thing for an ordinance to thee and to thy sons for ever.

^{25} *And it shall come to pass, when ye be come to the land which the Lord will give you, according as he hath promised, that ye shall keep this service.*

^{26} *And it shall come to pass, when your children shall say unto you, What mean ye by this service?*

^{27}**That ye shall say, It is the sacrifice of the Lord's passover, who passed over the houses of the children of Israel in Egypt, when he smote the Egyptians, and delivered our houses. And the people bowed the head and worshipped.**

^{28} *And the children of Israel went away, and did as the Lord had commanded Moses and Aaron, so did they.*

^{29} **And it came to pass, that at midnight the Lord smote all the firstborn in the land of Egypt, from the firstborn of Pharaoh that sat on his throne unto the firstborn of the captive that was in the dungeon; and all the firstborn of cattle.**

^{30} *And Pharaoh rose up in the night, he, and all his servants, and all the Egyptians; and there was a great cry in Egypt;* **for there was not a house where there was not one dead.**

&

Exodus 32: 26 - 29 KJV

^{26} *Then Moses stood in the gate of the camp, and said,* **Who is on the Lord's side? let him come unto me**. *And all the sons of Levi gathered themselves together unto him.*

^{27} **And he said unto them, Thus saith the Lord God of Israel, Put every man his sword by his side, and go in and out from gate to gate throughout the camp, and slay every man his brother, and every man his companion, and every man his neighbour.**

²⁸ And the children of Levi did according to the word of Moses: and there fell of the people that day about three thousand men.

²⁹ For Moses had said, Consecrate yourselves today to the Lord, even every man upon his son, and upon his brother; that he may bestow upon you a blessing this day.

Deuteronomy 13 KJV

13 If there arise among you a prophet, or a dreamer of dreams, and giveth thee a sign or a wonder,

² And the sign or the wonder come to pass, whereof he spake unto thee, saying, Let us go after other gods, which thou hast not known, and let us serve them;

³ Thou shalt not hearken unto the words of that prophet, or that dreamer of dreams: for the Lord your God proveth you, to know whether ye love the Lord your God with all your heart and with all your soul.

⁴ Ye shall walk after the Lord your God, and fear him, and keep his commandments, and obey his voice, and ye shall serve him, and cleave unto him.

⁵ And that prophet, or that dreamer of dreams, shall be put to death; because he hath spoken to turn you away from the Lord your God, which brought you out of the land of Egypt, and redeemed you out of the house of bondage, to thrust thee out of the way which the Lord thy God commanded thee to walk in. So shalt thou put the evil away from the midst of thee.

⁶ If thy brother, the son of thy mother, or thy son, or thy daughter, or the wife of thy bosom, or thy friend, which is as thine own soul, entice thee secretly, saying, Let us go and serve other gods, which thou hast not known, thou, nor thy fathers;

⁷ Namely, of the gods of the people which are round about you, nigh unto thee, or far off from thee, from the one end of the earth even unto the other end of the earth;

⁸ Thou shalt not consent unto him, nor hearken unto him; neither shall thine eye pity him, neither shalt thou spare, neither shalt thou conceal him:

⁹ But thou shalt surely kill him; thine hand shall be first upon him to put him to death, and afterwards the hand of all the people.

¹⁰ And thou shalt stone him with stones, that he die; because he hath sought to thrust thee away from the Lord thy God, which brought thee out of the land of Egypt, from the house of bondage.

¹¹ And all Israel shall hear, and fear, and shall do no more any such wickedness as this is among you.

¹² If thou shalt hear say in one of thy cities, which the Lord thy God hath given thee to dwell there, saying,

¹³ Certain men, the children of Belial, are gone out from among you, and have withdrawn the inhabitants of their city, saying, Let us go and serve other gods, which ye have not known;

¹⁴ Then shalt thou enquire, and make search, and ask diligently; and, behold, if it be truth, and the thing certain, that such abomination is wrought among you;

¹⁵ Thou shalt surely smite the inhabitants of that city with the edge of the sword, destroying it utterly, and all that is therein, and the cattle thereof, with the edge of the sword.

¹⁶ And thou shalt gather all the spoil of it into the midst of the street thereof, and shalt burn with fire the city, and all the spoil

thereof every whit, for the Lord thy God: and it shall be an heap
for ever; it shall not be built again.

[17] *And there shall cleave nought of the cursed thing to thine hand:*
that the Lord may turn from the fierceness of his anger, and shew
thee mercy, and have compassion upon thee, and multiply thee, as he
hath sworn unto thy fathers;

[18] *When thou shalt hearken to the voice of the Lord thy God, to keep*
all his commandments which I command thee this day, to do that
which is right in the eyes of the Lord thy God.

&

Numbers 31: 1-31 KJV

31 And the Lord spake unto Moses, saying,

[2] *Avenge the children of Israel of the Midianites: afterward shalt*
thou be gathered unto thy people.

[3] *And Moses spake unto the people, saying, Arm some of yourselves*
unto the war, and let them go against the Midianites, and avenge
the Lord of Midian.

[4] *Of every tribe a thousand, throughout all the tribes of Israel, shall*
ye send to the war.

[5] *So there were delivered out of the thousands of Israel, a thousand*
of every tribe, twelve thousand armed for war.

[6] *And Moses sent them to the war, a thousand of every tribe, them*
and Phinehas the son of Eleazar the priest, to the war, with the holy
instruments, and the trumpets to blow in his hand.

7 And they warred against the Midianites, as the Lord commanded Moses; and they slew all the males.

8 And they slew the kings of Midian, beside the rest of them that were slain; namely, Evi, and Rekem, and Zur, and Hur, and Reba, five kings of Midian: Balaam also the son of Beor they slew with the sword.

9 And the children of Israel took all the women of Midian captives, and their little ones, and took the spoil of all their cattle, and all their flocks, and all their goods.

10 And they burnt all their cities wherein they dwelt, and all their goodly castles, with fire.

11 And they took all the spoil, and all the prey, both of men and of beasts.

12 And they brought the captives, and the prey, and the spoil, unto Moses, and Eleazar the priest, and unto the congregation of the children of Israel, unto the camp at the plains of Moab, which are by Jordan near Jericho.

13 And Moses, and Eleazar the priest, and all the princes of the congregation, went forth to meet them without the camp.

14 And Moses was wroth with the officers of the host, with the captains over thousands, and captains over hundreds, which came from the battle.

15 And Moses said unto them, Have ye saved all the women alive?

16 Behold, these caused the children of Israel, through the counsel of Balaam, to commit trespass against the Lord in the matter of Peor, and there was a plague among the congregation of the Lord.

¹⁷ Now therefore kill every male among the little ones, and kill every woman that hath known man by lying with him.

¹⁸ But all the women children, that have not known a man by lying with him, keep alive for yourselves.

¹⁹ And do ye abide without the camp seven days: whosoever hath killed any person, and whosoever hath touched any slain, purify both yourselves and your captives on the third day, and on the seventh day.

²⁰ And purify all your raiment, and all that is made of skins, and all work of goats' hair, and all things made of wood.

²¹ And Eleazar the priest said unto the men of war which went to the battle, This is the ordinance of the law which the Lord commanded Moses;

²² Only the gold, and the silver, the brass, the iron, the tin, and the lead,

²³ Every thing that may abide the fire, ye shall make it go through the fire, and it shall be clean: nevertheless it shall be purified with the water of separation: and all that abideth not the fire ye shall make go through the water.

²⁴ And ye shall wash your clothes on the seventh day, and ye shall be clean, and afterward ye shall come into the camp.

²⁵ And the Lord spake unto Moses, saying,

²⁶ Take the sum of the prey that was taken, both of man and of beast, thou, and Eleazar the priest, and the chief fathers of the congregation:

²⁷ And divide the prey into two parts; between them that took the war upon them, who went out to battle, and between all the congregation:

²⁸ And levy a tribute unto the Lord of the men of war which went out to battle: one soul of five hundred, both of the persons, and of the beeves, and of the asses, and of the sheep:

²⁹ Take it of their half, and give it unto Eleazar the priest, for an heave offering of the Lord.

³⁰ And of the children of Israel's half, thou shalt take one portion of fifty, of the persons, of the beeves, of the asses, and of the flocks, of all manner of beasts, and give them unto the Levites, which keep the charge of the tabernacle of the Lord.

³¹ And Moses and Eleazar the priest did as the Lord commanded Moses.

Or maybe blood sacrifice of animals, children, and his own "son?" (Exodus 20:24, Hebrews 9:22, Leviticus 1:9, Judges 11:30–39, Hebrews 10:10)

Exodus 20 KJV

20 And God spake all these words, saying,

[2] I am the Lord thy God, which have brought thee out of the land of Egypt, out of the house of bondage.

[3] Thou shalt have no other gods before me.

[4] Thou shalt not make unto thee any graven image, or any likeness of any thing that is in heaven above, or that is in the earth beneath, or that is in the water under the earth.

[5] Thou shalt not bow down thyself to them, nor serve them: for I the Lord thy God am a jealous God, visiting the iniquity of the fathers upon the children unto the third and fourth generation of them that hate me;

[6] And shewing mercy unto thousands of them that love me, and keep my commandments.

[7] Thou shalt not take the name of the Lord thy God in vain; for the Lord will not hold him guiltless that taketh his name in vain.

[8] Remember the sabbath day, to keep it holy.

[9] Six days shalt thou labour, and do all thy work:

[10] But the seventh day is the sabbath of the Lord thy God: in it thou shalt not do any work, thou, nor thy son, nor thy daughter, thy manservant, nor thy maidservant, nor thy cattle, nor thy stranger that is within thy gates:

11 For in six days the Lord made heaven and earth, the sea, and all that in them is, and rested the seventh day: wherefore the Lord blessed the sabbath day, and hallowed it.

12 Honour thy father and thy mother: that thy days may be long upon the land which the Lord thy God giveth thee.

13 Thou shalt not kill.

14 Thou shalt not commit adultery.

15 Thou shalt not steal.

16 Thou shalt not bear false witness against thy neighbour.

17 Thou shalt not covet thy neighbour's house, thou shalt not covet thy neighbour's wife, nor his manservant, nor his maidservant, nor his ox, nor his ass, nor any thing that is thy neighbour's.

18 And all the people saw the thunderings, and the lightnings, and the noise of the trumpet, and the mountain smoking: and when the people saw it, they removed, and stood afar off.

19 And they said unto Moses, Speak thou with us, and we will hear: but let not God speak with us, lest we die.

20 And Moses said unto the people, Fear not: for God is come to prove you, and that his fear may be before your faces, that ye sin not.

21 And the people stood afar off, and Moses drew near unto the thick darkness where God was.

22 And the Lord said unto Moses, Thus thou shalt say unto the children of Israel, Ye have seen that I have talked with you from heaven.

23 Ye shall not make with me gods of silver, neither shall ye make unto you gods of gold.

*24 An altar of earth thou shalt make unto me, and shalt sacrifice thereon thy burnt offerings, and thy peace offerings, **thy sheep, and thine oxen**: in all places where I record my name I will come unto thee, and I will bless thee.*

25 And if thou wilt make me an altar of stone, thou shalt not build it of hewn stone: for if thou lift up thy tool upon it, thou hast polluted it.

26 Neither shalt thou go up by steps unto mine altar, that thy nakedness be not discovered thereon.

&

Hebrews 9 King James Version

9 Then verily the first covenant had also ordinances of divine service, and a worldly sanctuary.

2 For there was a tabernacle made; the first, wherein was the candlestick, and the table, and the shewbread; which is called the sanctuary.

3 And after the second veil, the tabernacle which is called the Holiest of all;

4 Which had the golden censer, and the ark of the covenant overlaid round about with gold, wherein was the golden pot that had manna, and Aaron's rod that budded, and the tables of the covenant;

5 And over it the cherubims of glory shadowing the mercyseat; of which we cannot now speak particularly.

⁶ Now when these things were thus ordained, the priests went always into the first tabernacle, accomplishing the service of God.

⁷ But into the second went the high priest alone once every year, not without blood, which he offered for himself, and for the errors of the people:

⁸ The Holy Ghost this signifying, that the way into the holiest of all was not yet made manifest, while as the first tabernacle was yet standing:

⁹ Which was a figure for the time then present, in which were offered both gifts and sacrifices, that could not make him that did the service perfect, as pertaining to the conscience;

¹⁰ Which stood only in meats and drinks, and divers washings, and carnal ordinances, imposed on them until the time of reformation.

¹¹ But Christ being come an high priest of good things to come, by a greater and more perfect tabernacle, not made with hands, that is to say, not of this building;

¹² Neither by the blood of goats and calves, but by his own blood he entered in once into the holy place, having obtained eternal redemption for us.

¹³ For if the blood of bulls and of goats, and the ashes of an heifer sprinkling the unclean, sanctifieth to the purifying of the flesh:

¹⁴ How much more shall the blood of Christ, who through the eternal Spirit offered himself without spot to God, purge your conscience from dead works to serve the living God?

¹⁵ And for this cause he is the mediator of the new testament, that by means of death, for the redemption of the transgressions that were under the first testament, they which are called might receive the promise of eternal inheritance.

16 For where a testament is, there must also of necessity be the death of the testator.

17 For a testament is of force after men are dead: otherwise it is of no strength at all while the testator liveth.

18 Whereupon neither the first testament was dedicated without blood.

19 For when Moses had spoken every precept to all the people according to the law, he took the blood of calves and of goats, with water, and scarlet wool, and hyssop, and sprinkled both the book, and all the people,

20 Saying, This is the blood of the testament which God hath enjoined unto you.

21 Moreover he sprinkled with blood both the tabernacle, and all the vessels of the ministry.

22 And almost all things are by the law purged with blood; and without shedding of blood is no remission.

23 It was therefore necessary that the patterns of things in the heavens should be purified with these; but the heavenly things themselves with better sacrifices than these.

24 For Christ is not entered into the holy places made with hands, which are the figures of the true; but into heaven itself, now to appear in the presence of God for us:

25 Nor yet that he should offer himself often, as the high priest entereth into the holy place every year with blood of others;

^{26} *For then must he often have suffered since the foundation of the world: but now once in the end of the world hath he appeared to put away sin by the sacrifice of himself.*

^{27} *And as it is appointed unto men once to die, but after this the judgment:*

^{28} *So Christ was once offered to bear the sins of many; and unto them that look for him shall he appear the second time without sin unto salvation.*

Hebrews 10 King James Version

10 *For the law having a shadow of good things to come, and not the very image of the things, can never with those sacrifices which they offered year by year continually make the comers thereunto perfect.*

^{2} *For then would they not have ceased to be offered? because that the worshippers once purged should have had no more conscience of sins.*

^{3} *But in those sacrifices there is a remembrance again made of sins every year.*

^{4} *For it is not possible that the blood of bulls and of goats should take away sins.*

^{5} *Wherefore when he cometh into the world, he saith, Sacrifice and offering thou wouldest not, but a body hast thou prepared me:*

^{6} *In burnt offerings and sacrifices for sin thou hast had no pleasure.*

⁷ Then said I, Lo, I come (in the volume of the book it is written of me,) to do thy will, O God.

⁸ Above when he said, Sacrifice and offering and burnt offerings and offering for sin thou wouldest not, neither hadst pleasure therein; which are offered by the law;

⁹ Then said he, Lo, I come to do thy will, O God. He taketh away the first, that he may establish the second.

¹⁰ By the which will we are sanctified through the offering of the body of Jesus Christ once for all.

¹¹ And every priest standeth daily ministering and offering oftentimes the same sacrifices, which can never take away sins:

¹² But this man, after he had offered one sacrifice for sins for ever, sat down on the right hand of God;

¹³ From henceforth expecting till his enemies be made his footstool.

¹⁴ For by one offering he hath perfected for ever them that are sanctified.

¹⁵ Whereof the Holy Ghost also is a witness to us: for after that he had said before,

¹⁶ This is the covenant that I will make with them after those days, saith the Lord, I will put my laws into their hearts, and in their minds will I write them;

¹⁷ And their sins and iniquities will I remember no more.

¹⁸ Now where remission of these is, there is no more offering for sin.

19 Having therefore, brethren, boldness to enter into the holiest by the blood of Jesus,

20 By a new and living way, which he hath consecrated for us, through the veil, that is to say, his flesh;

21 And having an high priest over the house of God;

22 Let us draw near with a true heart in full assurance of faith, having our hearts sprinkled from an evil conscience, and our bodies washed with pure water.

23 Let us hold fast the profession of our faith without wavering; (for he is faithful that promised;)

24 And let us consider one another to provoke unto love and to good works:

25 Not forsaking the assembling of ourselves together, as the manner of some is; but exhorting one another: and so much the more, as ye see the day approaching.

26 For if we sin wilfully after that we have received the knowledge of the truth, there remaineth no more sacrifice for sins,

27 But a certain fearful looking for of judgment and fiery indignation, which shall devour the adversaries.

28 He that despised Moses' law died without mercy under two or three witnesses:

29 Of how much sorer punishment, suppose ye, shall he be thought worthy, who hath trodden under foot the Son of God, and hath counted the blood of the covenant, wherewith he was sanctified, an unholy thing, and hath done despite unto the Spirit of grace?

³⁰ For we know him that hath said, Vengeance belongeth unto me, I will recompense, saith the Lord. And again, The Lord shall judge his people.

³¹ It is a fearful thing to fall into the hands of the living God.

³² But call to remembrance the former days, in which, after ye were illuminated, ye endured a great fight of afflictions;

³³ Partly, whilst ye were made a gazingstock both by reproaches and afflictions; and partly, whilst ye became companions of them that were so used.

³⁴ For ye had compassion of me in my bonds, and took joyfully the spoiling of your goods, knowing in yourselves that ye have in heaven a better and an enduring substance.

³⁵ Cast not away therefore your confidence, which hath great recompence of reward.

³⁶ For ye have need of patience, that, after ye have done the will of God, ye might receive the promise.

³⁷ For yet a little while, and he that shall come will come, and will not tarry.

³⁸ Now the just shall live by faith: but if any man draw back, my soul shall have no pleasure in him.

³⁹ But we are not of them who draw back unto perdition; but of them that believe to the saving of the soul.

&

Leviticus 1 King James Version

1 And the Lord called unto Moses, and spake unto him out of the tabernacle of the congregation, saying,

2 Speak unto the children of Israel, and say unto them, If any man of you bring an offering unto the Lord, ye shall bring your offering of the cattle, even of the herd, and of the flock.

3 If his offering be a burnt sacrifice of the herd, let him offer a male without blemish: he shall offer it of his own voluntary will at the door of the tabernacle of the congregation before the Lord.

4 And he shall put his hand upon the head of the burnt offering; and it shall be accepted for him to make atonement for him.

5 And he shall kill the bullock before the Lord: and the priests, Aaron's sons, shall bring the blood, and sprinkle the blood round about upon the altar that is by the door of the tabernacle of the congregation.

6 And he shall flay the burnt offering, and cut it into his pieces.

7 And the sons of Aaron the priest shall put fire upon the altar, and lay the wood in order upon the fire:

8 And the priests, Aaron's sons, shall lay the parts, the head, and the fat, in order upon the wood that is on the fire which is upon the altar:

9 But his inwards and his legs shall he wash in water: and the priest shall burn all on the altar, to be a burnt sacrifice, an offering made by fire, of a sweet savour unto the Lord.

10 And if his offering be of the flocks, namely, of the sheep, or of the goats, for a burnt sacrifice; he shall bring it a male without blemish.

¹¹ And he shall kill it on the side of the altar northward before the Lord: and the priests, Aaron's sons, shall sprinkle his blood round about upon the altar.

¹² And he shall cut it into his pieces, with his head and his fat: and the priest shall lay them in order on the wood that is on the fire which is upon the altar:

¹³ But he shall wash the inwards and the legs with water: and the priest shall bring it all, and burn it upon the altar: it is a burnt sacrifice, an offering made by fire, of a sweet savour unto the Lord.

¹⁴ And if the burnt sacrifice for his offering to the Lord be of fowls, then he shall bring his offering of turtledoves, or of young pigeons.

¹⁵ And the priest shall bring it unto the altar, and wring off his head, and burn it on the altar; and the blood thereof shall be wrung out at the side of the altar:

¹⁶ And he shall pluck away his crop with his feathers, and cast it beside the altar on the east part, by the place of the ashes:

¹⁷ And he shall cleave it with the wings thereof, but shall not divide it asunder: and the priest shall burn it upon the altar, upon the wood that is upon the fire: it is a burnt sacrifice, an offering made by fire, of a sweet savour unto the Lord.

&

Judges 11:30–39 KJV

³⁰ And Jephthah vowed a vow unto the Lord, and said, If thou shalt without fail deliver the children of Ammon into mine hands,

31 Then it shall be, that whatsoever cometh forth of the doors of my house to meet me, when I return in peace from the children of Ammon, shall surely be the Lord's, and I will offer it up for a burnt offering.

32 So Jephthah passed over unto the children of Ammon to fight against them; and the Lord delivered them into his hands.

33 And he smote them from Aroer, even till thou come to Minnith, even twenty cities, and unto the plain of the vineyards, with a very great slaughter. Thus the children of Ammon were subdued before the children of Israel.

34 And Jephthah came to Mizpeh unto his house, and, behold, his daughter came out to meet him with timbrels and with dances: and she was his only child; beside her he had neither son nor daughter.

35 And it came to pass, when he saw her, that he rent his clothes, and said, Alas, my daughter! thou hast brought me very low, and thou art one of them that trouble me: for I have opened my mouth unto the Lord, and I cannot go back.

36 And she said unto him, My father, if thou hast opened thy mouth unto the Lord, do to me according to that which hath proceeded out of thy mouth; forasmuch as the Lord hath taken vengeance for thee of thine enemies, even of the children of Ammon.

37 And she said unto her father, Let this thing be done for me: let me alone two months, that I may go up and down upon the mountains, and bewail my virginity, I and my fellows.

38 And he said, Go. And he sent her away for two months: and she went with her companions, and bewailed her virginity upon the mountains.

[39]And it came to pass at the end of two months, that she returned unto her father, who did with her according to his vow which he had vowed: and she knew no man. And it was a custom in Israel,

Revelation 9 King James Version

9 And the fifth angel sounded, and I saw a star fall from heaven unto the earth: and to him was given the key of the bottomless pit.

2 And he opened the bottomless pit; and there arose a smoke out of the pit, as the smoke of a great furnace; and the sun and the air were darkened by reason of the smoke of the pit.

3 And there came out of the smoke locusts upon the earth: and unto them was given power, as the scorpions of the earth have power.

4 And it was commanded them that they should not hurt the grass of the earth, neither any green thing, neither any tree; but only those men which have not the seal of God in their foreheads.

5 And to them it was given that they should not kill them, but that they should be tormented five months: and their torment was as the torment of a scorpion, when he striketh a man.

6 And in those days shall men seek death, and shall not find it; and shall desire to die, and death shall flee from them.

7 And the shapes of the locusts were like unto horses prepared unto battle; and on their heads were as it were crowns like gold, and their faces were as the faces of men.

8 And they had hair as the hair of women, and their teeth were as the teeth of lions.

9 And they had breastplates, as it were breastplates of iron; and the sound of their wings was as the sound of chariots of many horses running to battle.

10 And they had tails like unto scorpions, and there were stings in their tails: and their power was to hurt men five months.

11 And they had a king over them, which is the angel of the bottomless pit, whose name in the Hebrew tongue is Abaddon, but in the Greek tongue hath his name Apollyon.

12 One woe is past; and, behold, there come two woes more hereafter.

13 And the sixth angel sounded, and I heard a voice from the four horns of the golden altar which is before God,

14 Saying to the sixth angel which had the trumpet, Loose the four angels which are bound in the great river Euphrates.

15 And the four angels were loosed, which were prepared for an hour, and a day, and a month, and a year, for to slay the third part of men.

16 And the number of the army of the horsemen were two hundred thousand thousand: and I heard the number of them.

17 And thus I saw the horses in the vision, and them that sat on them, having breastplates of fire, and of jacinth, and brimstone: and the heads of the horses were as the heads of lions; and out of their mouths issued fire and smoke and brimstone.

18 By these three was the third part of men killed, by the fire, and by the smoke, and by the brimstone, which issued out of their mouths.

19 For their power is in their mouth, and in their tails: for their tails were like unto serpents, and had heads, and with them they do hurt.

20 And the rest of the men which were not killed by these plagues yet repented not of the works of their hands, that they should not worship devils, and idols of gold, and silver, and brass, and stone, and of wood: which neither can see, nor hear, nor walk:

[21] Neither repented they of their murders, nor of their sorceries, nor of their fornication, nor of their thefts.

&

Revelation 20 King James Version

20 And I saw an angel come down from heaven, having the key of the bottomless pit and a great chain in his hand.

[2] And he laid hold on the dragon, that old serpent, which is the Devil, and Satan, and bound him a thousand years,

[3] And cast him into the bottomless pit, and shut him up, and set a seal upon him, that he should deceive the nations no more, till the thousand years should be fulfilled: and after that he must be loosed a little season.

[4] And I saw thrones, and they sat upon them, and judgment was given unto them: and I saw the souls of them that were beheaded for the witness of Jesus, and for the word of God, and which had not worshipped the beast, neither his image, neither had received his mark upon their foreheads, or in their hands; and they lived and reigned with Christ a thousand years.

[5] But the rest of the dead lived not again until the thousand years were finished. This is the first resurrection.

[6] Blessed and holy is he that hath part in the first resurrection: on such the second death hath no power, but they shall be priests of God and of Christ, and shall reign with him a thousand years.

⁷ And when the thousand years are expired, Satan shall be loosed out of his prison,

⁸ And shall go out to deceive the nations which are in the four quarters of the earth, Gog, and Magog, to gather them together to battle: the number of whom is as the sand of the sea.

⁹ And they went up on the breadth of the earth, and compassed the camp of the saints about, and the beloved city: and fire came down from God out of heaven, and devoured them.

¹⁰ And the devil that deceived them was cast into the lake of fire and brimstone, where the beast and the false prophet are, and shall be tormented day and night for ever and ever.

¹¹ And I saw a great white throne, and him that sat on it, from whose face the earth and the heaven fled away; and there was found no place for them.

¹² And I saw the dead, small and great, stand before God; and the books were opened: and another book was opened, which is the book of life: and the dead were judged out of those things which were written in the books, according to their works.

¹³ And the sea gave up the dead which were in it; and death and hell delivered up the dead which were in them: and they were judged every man according to their works.

¹⁴ And death and hell were cast into the lake of fire. This is the second death.

¹⁵ And whosoever was not found written in the book of life was cast into the lake of fire.

2 Samuel 12:7-31 KJV

[7] And Nathan said to David, Thou art the man. Thus saith the Lord God of Israel, I anointed thee king over Israel, and I delivered thee out of the hand of Saul;

[8] And I gave thee thy master's house, and thy master's wives into thy bosom, and gave thee the house of Israel and of Judah; and if that had been too little, I would moreover have given unto thee such and such things.

[9] Wherefore hast thou despised the commandment of the Lord, to do evil in his sight? thou hast killed Uriah the Hittite with the sword, and hast taken his wife to be thy wife, and hast slain him with the sword of the children of Ammon.

[10] Now therefore the sword shall never depart from thine house; because thou hast despised me, and hast taken the wife of Uriah the Hittite to be thy wife.

[11] Thus saith the Lord, Behold, I will raise up evil against thee out of thine own house, and I will take thy wives before thine eyes, and give them unto thy neighbour, and he shall lie with thy wives in the sight of this sun.

[12] For thou didst it secretly: but I will do this thing before all Israel, and before the sun.

[13] And David said unto Nathan, I have sinned against the Lord. And Nathan said unto David, The Lord also hath put away thy sin; thou shalt not die.

¹⁴ Howbeit, because by this deed thou hast given great occasion to the enemies of the Lord to blaspheme, the child also that is born unto thee shall surely die.

¹⁵ And Nathan departed unto his house. And the Lord struck the child that Uriah's wife bare unto David, and it was very sick.

¹⁶ David therefore besought God for the child; and David fasted, and went in, and lay all night upon the earth.

¹⁷ And the elders of his house arose, and went to him, to raise him up from the earth: but he would not, neither did he eat bread with them.

¹⁸ And it came to pass on the seventh day, that the child died. And the servants of David feared to tell him that the child was dead: for they said, Behold, while the child was yet alive, we spake unto him, and he would not hearken unto our voice: how will he then vex himself, if we tell him that the child is dead?

¹⁹ But when David saw that his servants whispered, David perceived that the child was dead: therefore David said unto his servants, Is the child dead? And they said, He is dead.

²⁰ Then David arose from the earth, and washed, and anointed himself, and changed his apparel, and came into the house of the Lord, and worshipped: then he came to his own house; and when he required, they set bread before him, and he did eat.

²¹ Then said his servants unto him, What thing is this that thou hast done? thou didst fast and weep for the child, while it was alive; but when the child was dead, thou didst rise and eat bread.

²² And he said, While the child was yet alive, I fasted and wept: for I said, Who can tell whether God will be gracious to me, that the child may live?

^{23} *But now he is dead, wherefore should I fast? can I bring him back again? I shall go to him, but he shall not return to me.*

^{24} *And David comforted Bathsheba his wife, and went in unto her, and lay with her: and she bare a son, and he called his name Solomon: and the Lord loved him.*

^{25} *And he sent by the hand of Nathan the prophet; and he called his name Jedidiah, because of the Lord.*

^{26} *And Joab fought against Rabbah of the children of Ammon, and took the royal city.*

^{27} *And Joab sent messengers to David, and said, I have fought against Rabbah, and have taken the city of waters.*

^{28} *Now therefore gather the rest of the people together, and encamp against the city, and take it: lest I take the city, and it be called after my name.*

^{29} *And David gathered all the people together, and went to Rabbah, and fought against it, and took it.*

^{30} *And he took their king's crown from off his head, the weight whereof was a talent of gold with the precious stones: and it was set on David's head. And he brought forth the spoil of the city in great abundance.*

^{31} *And he brought forth the people that were therein, and put them under saws, and under harrows of iron, and under axes of iron, and made them pass through the brick-kiln: and thus did he unto all the cities of the children of Ammon. So David and all the people returned unto Jerusalem.*

&

2 Kings 2 King James Version

2 And it came to pass, when the Lord would take up Elijah into heaven by a whirlwind, that Elijah went with Elisha from Gilgal.

2 And Elijah said unto Elisha, Tarry here, I pray thee; for the Lord hath sent me to Bethel. And Elisha said unto him, As the Lord liveth, and as thy soul liveth, I will not leave thee. So they went down to Bethel.

3 And the sons of the prophets that were at Bethel came forth to Elisha, and said unto him, Knowest thou that the Lord will take away thy master from thy head to day? And he said, Yea, I know it; hold ye your peace.

4 And Elijah said unto him, Elisha, tarry here, I pray thee; for the Lord hath sent me to Jericho. And he said, As the Lord liveth, and as thy soul liveth, I will not leave thee. So they came to Jericho.

5 And the sons of the prophets that were at Jericho came to Elisha, and said unto him, Knowest thou that the Lord will take away thy master from thy head to day? And he answered, Yea, I know it; hold ye your peace.

6 And Elijah said unto him, Tarry, I pray thee, here; for the Lord hath sent me to Jordan. And he said, As the Lord liveth, and as thy soul liveth, I will not leave thee. And they two went on.

7 And fifty men of the sons of the prophets went, and stood to view afar off: and they two stood by Jordan.

8 And Elijah took his mantle, and wrapped it together, and smote the waters, and they were divided hither and thither, so that they two went over on dry ground.

⁹ And it came to pass, when they were gone over, that Elijah said unto Elisha, Ask what I shall do for thee, before I be taken away from thee. And Elisha said, I pray thee, let a double portion of thy spirit be upon me.

¹⁰ And he said, Thou hast asked a hard thing: nevertheless, if thou see me when I am taken from thee, it shall be so unto thee; but if not, it shall not be so.

¹¹ And it came to pass, as they still went on, and talked, that, behold, there appeared a chariot of fire, and horses of fire, and parted them both asunder; and Elijah went up by a whirlwind into heaven.

¹² And Elisha saw it, and he cried, My father, my father, the chariot of Israel, and the horsemen thereof. And he saw him no more: and he took hold of his own clothes, and rent them in two pieces.

¹³ He took up also the mantle of Elijah that fell from him, and went back, and stood by the bank of Jordan;

¹⁴ And he took the mantle of Elijah that fell from him, and smote the waters, and said, Where is the Lord God of Elijah? and when he also had smitten the waters, they parted hither and thither: and Elisha went over.

¹⁵ And when the sons of the prophets which were to view at Jericho saw him, they said, The spirit of Elijah doth rest on Elisha. And they came to meet him, and bowed themselves to the ground before him.

¹⁶ And they said unto him, Behold now, there be with thy servants fifty strong men; let them go, we pray thee, and seek thy master: lest peradventure the Spirit of the Lord hath taken him up, and cast him upon some mountain, or into some valley. And he said, Ye shall not send.

17 And when they urged him till he was ashamed, he said, Send. They sent therefore fifty men; and they sought three days, but found him not.

18 And when they came again to him, (for he tarried at Jericho,) he said unto them, Did I not say unto you, Go not?

19 And the men of the city said unto Elisha, Behold, I pray thee, the situation of this city is pleasant, as my lord seeth: but the water is naught, and the ground barren.

20 And he said, Bring me a new cruse, and put salt therein. And they brought it to him.

21 And he went forth unto the spring of the waters, and cast the salt in there, and said, Thus saith the Lord, I have healed these waters; there shall not be from thence any more death or barren land.

22 So the waters were healed unto this day, according to the saying of Elisha which he spake.

23 And he went up from thence unto Bethel: and as he was going up by the way, there came forth little children out of the city, and mocked him, and said unto him, Go up, thou bald head; go up, thou bald head.

24 And he turned back, and looked on them, and cursed them in the name of the Lord. And there came forth two she bears out of the wood, and tare forty and two children of them.

25 And he went from thence to mount Carmel, and from thence he returned to Samaria.

Joshua 11 King James Version

11 And it came to pass, when Jabin king of Hazor had heard those things, that he sent to Jobab king of Madon, and to the king of Shimron, and to the king of Achshaph,

² And to the kings that were on the north of the mountains, and of the plains south of Chinneroth, and in the valley, and in the borders of Dor on the west,

³ And to the Canaanite on the east and on the west, and to the Amorite, and the Hittite, and the Perizzite, and the Jebusite in the mountains, and to the Hivite under Hermon in the land of Mizpeh.

⁴ And they went out, they and all their hosts with them, much people, even as the sand that is upon the sea shore in multitude, with horses and chariots very many.

⁵ And when all these kings were met together, they came and pitched together at the waters of Merom, to fight against Israel.

⁶ And the Lord said unto Joshua, Be not afraid because of them: for to morrow about this time will I deliver them up all slain before Israel: thou shalt hough their horses, and burn their chariots with fire.

⁷ So Joshua came, and all the people of war with him, against them by the waters of Merom suddenly; and they fell upon them.

⁸ And the Lord delivered them into the hand of Israel, who smote them, and chased them unto great Zidon, and unto Misrephothmaim, and unto the valley of Mizpeh eastward; and they smote them, until they left them none remaining.

⁹ And Joshua did unto them as the Lord bade him: he houghed their horses, and burnt their chariots with fire.

¹⁰ And Joshua at that time turned back, and took Hazor, and smote the king thereof with the sword: for Hazor beforetime was the head of all those kingdoms.

¹¹ And they smote all the souls that were therein with the edge of the sword, utterly destroying them: there was not any left to breathe: and he burnt Hazor with fire.

¹² And all the cities of those kings, and all the kings of them, did Joshua take, and smote them with the edge of the sword, and he utterly destroyed them, as Moses the servant of the Lord commanded.

¹³ But as for the cities that stood still in their strength, Israel burned none of them, save Hazor only; that did Joshua burn.

¹⁴ And all the spoil of these cities, and the cattle, the children of Israel took for a prey unto themselves; but every man they smote with the edge of the sword, until they had destroyed them, neither left they any to breathe.

¹⁵ As the Lord commanded Moses his servant, so did Moses command Joshua, and so did Joshua; he left nothing undone of all that the Lord commanded Moses.

¹⁶ So Joshua took all that land, the hills, and all the south country, and all the land of Goshen, and the valley, and the plain, and the mountain of Israel, and the valley of the same;

¹⁷ Even from the mount Halak, that goeth up to Seir, even unto Baalgad in the valley of Lebanon under mount Hermon: and all their kings he took, and smote them, and slew them.

¹⁸ Joshua made war a long time with all those kings.

¹⁹ There was not a city that made peace with the children of Israel, save the Hivites the inhabitants of Gibeon: all other they took in battle.

²⁰ For it was of the Lord to harden their hearts, that they should come against Israel in battle, that he might destroy them utterly, and that they might have no favour, but that he might destroy them, as the Lord commanded Moses.

²¹ And at that time came Joshua, and cut off the Anakims from the mountains, from Hebron, from Debir, from Anab, and from all the mountains of Judah, and from all the mountains of Israel: Joshua destroyed them utterly with their cities.

²² There was none of the Anakims left in the land of the children of Israel: only in Gaza, in Gath, and in Ashdod, there remained.

²³ So Joshua took the whole land, according to all that the Lord said unto Moses; and Joshua gave it for an inheritance unto Israel according to their divisions by their tribes. And the land rested from war.

&

Genesis 7:18-23 KJV

¹⁸ And the waters prevailed, and were increased greatly upon the earth; and the ark went upon the face of the waters.

¹⁹ And the waters prevailed exceedingly upon the earth; and all the high hills, that were under the whole heaven, were covered.

²⁰ Fifteen cubits upward did the waters prevail; and the mountains were covered.

21 And all flesh died that moved upon the earth, both of fowl, and of cattle, and of beast, and of every creeping thing that creepeth upon the earth, and every man:

22 All in whose nostrils was the breath of life, of all that was in the dry land, died.

23 And every living substance was destroyed which was upon the face of the ground, both man, and cattle, and the creeping things, and the fowl of the heaven; and they were destroyed from the earth: and Noah only remained alive, and they that were with him in the ark.

Deuteronomy 20:13-14 KJV

20 When thou goest out to battle against thine enemies, and seest horses, and chariots, and a people more than thou, be not afraid of them: for the Lord thy God is with thee, which brought thee up out of the land of Egypt.

2 And it shall be, when ye are come nigh unto the battle, that the priest shall approach and speak unto the people,

3 And shall say unto them, Hear, O Israel, ye approach this day unto battle against your enemies: let not your hearts faint, fear not, and do not tremble, neither be ye terrified because of them;

4 For the Lord your God is he that goeth with you, to fight for you against your enemies, to save you.

5 And the officers shall speak unto the people, saying, What man is there that hath built a new house, and hath not dedicated it? let him go and return to his house, lest he die in the battle, and another man dedicate it.

6 And what man is he that hath planted a vineyard, and hath not yet eaten of it? let him also go and return unto his house, lest he die in the battle, and another man eat of it.

7 And what man is there that hath betrothed a wife, and hath not taken her? let him go and return unto his house, lest he die in the battle, and another man take her.

8 And the officers shall speak further unto the people, and they shall say, What man is there that is fearful and fainthearted? let him go and return unto his house, lest his brethren's heart faint as well as his heart.

9 And it shall be, when the officers have made an end of speaking unto the people that they shall make captains of the armies to lead the people.

10 When thou comest nigh unto a city to fight against it, then proclaim peace unto it.

11 And it shall be, if it make thee answer of peace, and open unto thee, then it shall be, that all the people that is found therein shall be tributaries unto thee, and they shall serve thee.

12 And if it will make no peace with thee, but will make war against thee, then thou shalt besiege it:

13 And when the Lord thy God hath delivered it into thine hands, thou shalt smite every male thereof with the edge of the sword:

14 But the women, and the little ones, and the cattle, and all that is in the city, even all the spoil thereof, shalt thou take unto thyself; and thou shalt eat the spoil of thine enemies, which the Lord thy God hath given thee.

15 Thus shalt thou do unto all the cities which are very far off from thee, which are not of the cities of these nations.

16 But of the cities of these people, which the Lord thy God doth give thee for an inheritance, thou shalt save alive nothing that breatheth:

17 But thou shalt utterly destroy them; namely, the Hittites, and the Amorites, the Canaanites, and the Perizzites, the Hivites, and the Jebusites; as the Lord thy God hath commanded thee:

18 That they teach you not to do after all their abominations, which they have done unto their gods; so should ye sin against the Lord your God.

¹⁹ When thou shalt besiege a city a long time, in making war against it to take it, thou shalt not destroy the trees thereof by forcing an axe against them: for thou mayest eat of them, and thou shalt not cut them down (for the tree of the field is man's life) to employ them in the siege:

²⁰ Only the trees which thou knowest that they be not trees for meat, thou shalt destroy and cut them down; and thou shalt build bulwarks against the city that maketh war with thee, until it be subdued.

&

Luke 19 KJV

19 And Jesus entered and passed through Jericho.

² And, behold, there was a man named Zacchaeus, which was the chief among the publicans, and he was rich.

³ And he sought to see Jesus who he was; and could not for the press, because he was little of stature.

⁴ And he ran before, and climbed up into a sycomore tree to see him: for he was to pass that way.

⁵ And when Jesus came to the place, he looked up, and saw him, and said unto him, Zacchaeus, make haste, and come down; for to day I must abide at thy house.

⁶ And he made haste, and came down, and received him joyfully.

⁷ And when they saw it, they all murmured, saying, That he was gone to be guest with a man that is a sinner.

⁸ And Zacchaeus stood, and said unto the Lord: Behold, Lord, the half of my goods I give to the poor; and if I have taken any thing from any man by false accusation, I restore him fourfold.

⁹ And Jesus said unto him, This day is salvation come to this house, forsomuch as he also is a son of Abraham.

¹⁰ For the Son of man is come to seek and to save that which was lost.

¹¹ And as they heard these things, he added and spake a parable, because he was nigh to Jerusalem, and because they thought that the kingdom of God should immediately appear.

¹² He said therefore, A certain nobleman went into a far country to receive for himself a kingdom, and to return.

¹³ And he called his ten servants, and delivered them ten pounds, and said unto them, Occupy till I come.

¹⁴ But his citizens hated him, and sent a message after him, saying, We will not have this man to reign over us.

¹⁵ And it came to pass, that when he was returned, having received the kingdom, then he commanded these servants to be called unto him, to whom he had given the money, that he might know how much every man had gained by trading.

¹⁶ Then came the first, saying, Lord, thy pound hath gained ten pounds.

¹⁷ And he said unto him, Well, thou good servant: because thou hast been faithful in a very little, have thou authority over ten cities.

¹⁸ And the second came, saying, Lord, thy pound hath gained five pounds.

¹⁹ And he said likewise to him, Be thou also over five cities.

²⁰ And another came, saying, Lord, behold, here is thy pound, which I have kept laid up in a napkin:

²¹ For I feared thee, because thou art an austere man: thou takest up that thou layedst not down, and reapest that thou didst not sow.

²² And he saith unto him, Out of thine own mouth will I judge thee, thou wicked servant. Thou knewest that I was an austere man, taking up that I laid not down, and reaping that I did not sow:

²³ Wherefore then gavest not thou my money into the bank, that at my coming I might have required mine own with usury?

²⁴ And he said unto them that stood by, Take from him the pound, and give it to him that hath ten pounds.

²⁵ (And they said unto him, Lord, he hath ten pounds.)

²⁶ For I say unto you, That unto every one which hath shall be given; and from him that hath not, even that he hath shall be taken away from him.

²⁷ But those mine enemies, which would not that I should reign over them, bring hither, and slay them before me.

²⁸ And when he had thus spoken, he went before, ascending up to Jerusalem.

²⁹ And it came to pass, when he was come nigh to Bethphage and Bethany, at the mount called the mount of Olives, he sent two of his disciples,

³⁰ *Saying, Go ye into the village over against you; in the which at your entering ye shall find a colt tied, whereon yet never man sat: loose him, and bring him hither.*

³¹ *And if any man ask you, Why do ye loose him? thus shall ye say unto him, Because the Lord hath need of him.*

³² *And they that were sent went their way, and found even as he had said unto them.*

³³ *And as they were loosing the colt, the owners thereof said unto them, Why loose ye the colt?*

³⁴ *And they said, The Lord hath need of him.*

³⁵ *And they brought him to Jesus: and they cast their garments upon the colt, and they set Jesus thereon.*

³⁶ *And as he went, they spread their clothes in the way.*

³⁷ *And when he was come nigh, even now at the descent of the mount of Olives, the whole multitude of the disciples began to rejoice and praise God with a loud voice for all the mighty works that they had seen;*

³⁸ *Saying, Blessed be the King that cometh in the name of the Lord: peace in heaven, and glory in the highest.*

³⁹ *And some of the Pharisees from among the multitude said unto him, Master, rebuke thy disciples.*

⁴⁰ *And he answered and said unto them, I tell you that, if these should hold their peace, the stones would immediately cry out.*

⁴¹ *And when he was come near, he beheld the city, and wept over it,*

⁴² Saying, If thou hadst known, even thou, at least in this thy day, the things which belong unto thy peace! but now they are hid from thine eyes.

⁴³ For the days shall come upon thee, that thine enemies shall cast a trench about thee, and compass thee round, and keep thee in on every side,

⁴⁴ And shall lay thee even with the ground, and thy children within thee; and they shall not leave in thee one stone upon another; because thou knewest not the time of thy visitation.

⁴⁵ And he went into the temple, and began to cast out them that sold therein, and them that bought;

⁴⁶ Saying unto them, It is written, My house is the house of prayer: but ye have made it a den of thieves.

⁴⁷ And he taught daily in the temple. But the chief priests and the scribes and the chief of the people sought to destroy him,

⁴⁸ And could not find what they might do: for all the people were very attentive to hear him.

Leviticus 25:44-46 King James Version

⁴⁴ Both thy bondmen, and thy bondmaids, which thou shalt have, shall be of the heathen that are round about you; of them shall ye buy bondmen and bondmaids.

⁴⁵ Moreover of the children of the strangers that do sojourn among you, of them shall ye buy, and of their families that are with you, which they begat in your land: and they shall be your possession.

⁴⁶ And ye shall take them as an inheritance for your children after you, to inherit them for a possession; they shall be your bondmen for ever: but over your brethren the children of Israel, ye shall not rule one over another with rigour.

&

Exodus 21 King James Version

21 Now these are the judgments which thou shalt set before them.

² If thou buy an Hebrew servant, six years he shall serve: and in the seventh he shall go out free for nothing.

³ If he came in by himself, he shall go out by himself: if he were married, then his wife shall go out with him.

4 If his master have given him a wife, and she have born him sons or daughters; the wife and her children shall be her master's, and he shall go out by himself.

5 And if the servant shall plainly say, I love my master, my wife, and my children; I will not go out free:

6 Then his master shall bring him unto the judges; he shall also bring him to the door, or unto the door post; and his master shall bore his ear through with an aul; and he shall serve him for ever.

7 And if a man sell his daughter to be a maidservant, she shall not go out as the menservants do.

8 If she please not her master, who hath betrothed her to himself, then shall he let her be redeemed: to sell her unto a strange nation he shall have no power, seeing he hath dealt deceitfully with her.

9 And if he have betrothed her unto his son, he shall deal with her after the manner of daughters.

10 If he take him another wife; her food, her raiment, and her duty of marriage, shall he not diminish.

11 And if he do not these three unto her, then shall she go out free without money.

How about pedophilia, incest, and rape? (Genesis 3:20, Genesis 19:8 and 19:36, Judges 19: 23-29, Numbers 31:17-18, 2 Peter 2:7-8(in reference to Lot offering his daughters in Genesis 19:8), Deuteronomy 22:28-29(a raped virgin must marry her rapist)

Genesis 3: 17-24 KJV

17 And unto Adam he said, Because thou hast hearkened unto the voice of thy wife, and hast eaten of the tree, of which I commanded thee, saying, Thou shalt not eat of it: cursed is the ground for thy sake; in sorrow shalt thou eat of it all the days of thy life;

18 Thorns also and thistles shall it bring forth to thee; and thou shalt eat the herb of the field;

19 In the sweat of thy face shalt thou eat bread, till thou return unto the ground; for out of it wast thou taken: for dust thou art, and unto dust shalt thou return.

20 And Adam called his wife's name Eve; because she was the mother of all living.

21 Unto Adam also and to his wife did the Lord God make coats of skins, and clothed them.

22 And the Lord God said, Behold, the man is become as one of us, to know good and evil: and now, lest he put forth his hand, and take also of the tree of life, and eat, and live for ever:

23 Therefore the Lord God sent him forth from the garden of Eden, to till the ground from whence he was taken.

24 So he drove out the man; and he placed at the east of the garden of Eden Cherubims, and a flaming sword which turned every way, to keep the way of the tree of life.

&

Genesis 19 KJV

19 And there came two angels to Sodom at even; and Lot sat in the gate of Sodom: and Lot seeing them rose up to meet them; and he bowed himself with his face toward the ground;

2 And he said, Behold now, my lords, turn in, I pray you, into your servant's house, and tarry all night, and wash your feet, and ye shall rise up early, and go on your ways. And they said, Nay; but we will abide in the street all night.

3 And he pressed upon them greatly; and they turned in unto him, and entered into his house; and he made them a feast, and did bake unleavened bread, and they did eat.

4 But before they lay down, the men of the city, even the men of Sodom, compassed the house round, both old and young, all the people from every quarter:

5 And they called unto Lot, and said unto him, Where are the men which came in to thee this night? bring them out unto us, that we may know them.

6 And Lot went out at the door unto them, and shut the door after him,

7 And said, I pray you, brethren, do not so wickedly.

8 Behold now, I have two daughters which have not known man; let me, I pray you, bring them out unto you, and do ye to them as is good in your eyes: only unto these men do nothing; for therefore came they under the shadow of my roof.

⁹ And they said, Stand back. And they said again, This one fellow came in to sojourn, and he will needs be a judge: now will we deal worse with thee, than with them. And they pressed sore upon the man, even Lot, and came near to break the door.

¹⁰ But the men put forth their hand, and pulled Lot into the house to them, and shut to the door.

¹¹ And they smote the men that were at the door of the house with blindness, both small and great: so that they wearied themselves to find the door.

¹² And the men said unto Lot, Hast thou here any besides? son in law, and thy sons, and thy daughters, and whatsoever thou hast in the city, bring them out of this place:

¹³ For we will destroy this place, because the cry of them is waxen great before the face of the Lord; and the Lord hath sent us to destroy it.

¹⁴ And Lot went out, and spake unto his sons in law, which married his daughters, and said, Up, get you out of this place; for the Lord will destroy this city. But he seemed as one that mocked unto his sons in law.

¹⁵ And when the morning arose, then the angels hastened Lot, saying, Arise, take thy wife, and thy two daughters, which are here; lest thou be consumed in the iniquity of the city.

¹⁶ And while he lingered, the men laid hold upon his hand, and upon the hand of his wife, and upon the hand of his two daughters; the Lord being merciful unto him: and they brought him forth, and set him without the city.

17 And it came to pass, when they had brought them forth abroad, that he said, Escape for thy life; look not behind thee, neither stay thou in all the plain; escape to the mountain, lest thou be consumed.

18 And Lot said unto them, Oh, not so, my Lord:

19 Behold now, thy servant hath found grace in thy sight, and thou hast magnified thy mercy, which thou hast shewed unto me in saving my life; and I cannot escape to the mountain, lest some evil take me, and I die:

20 Behold now, this city is near to flee unto, and it is a little one: Oh, let me escape thither, (is it not a little one?) and my soul shall live.

21 And he said unto him, See, I have accepted thee concerning this thing also, that I will not overthrow this city, for the which thou hast spoken.

22 Haste thee, escape thither; for I cannot do anything till thou be come thither. Therefore the name of the city was called Zoar.

23 The sun was risen upon the earth when Lot entered into Zoar.

24 Then the Lord rained upon Sodom and upon Gomorrah brimstone and fire from the Lord out of heaven;

25 And he overthrew those cities, and all the plain, and all the inhabitants of the cities, and that which grew upon the ground.

26 But his wife looked back from behind him, and she became a pillar of salt.

27 And Abraham gat up early in the morning to the place where he stood before the Lord:

28 And he looked toward Sodom and Gomorrah, and toward all the land of the plain, and beheld, and, lo, the smoke of the country went up as the smoke of a furnace.

29 And it came to pass, when God destroyed the cities of the plain, that God remembered Abraham, and sent Lot out of the midst of the overthrow, when he overthrew the cities in the which Lot dwelt.

30 And Lot went up out of Zoar, and dwelt in the mountain, and his two daughters with him; for he feared to dwell in Zoar: and he dwelt in a cave, he and his two daughters.

31 And the firstborn said unto the younger, Our father is old, and there is not a man in the earth to come in unto us after the manner of all the earth:

32 Come, let us make our father drink wine, and we will lie with him, that we may preserve seed of our father.

33 And they made their father drink wine that night: and the firstborn went in, and lay with her father; and he perceived not when she lay down, nor when she arose.

34 And it came to pass on the morrow, that the firstborn said unto the younger, Behold, I lay yesternight with my father: let us make him drink wine this night also; and go thou in, and lie with him, that we may preserve seed of our father.

35 And they made their father drink wine that night also: and the younger arose, and lay with him; and he perceived not when she lay down, nor when she arose.

36 Thus were both the daughters of Lot with child by their father.

37 And the first born bare a son, and called his name Moab: the same is the father of the Moabites unto this day.

38 And the younger, she also bare a son, and called his name Benammi: the same is the father of the children of Ammon unto this day.

&

Judges 19:22-29 KJV

22 Now as they were making their hearts merry, behold, the men of the city, certain sons of Belial, beset the house round about, and beat at the door, and spake to the master of the house, the old man, saying, Bring forth the man that came into thine house, that we may know him.

23 And the man, the master of the house, went out unto them, and said unto them, Nay, my brethren, nay, I pray you, do not so wickedly; seeing that this man is come into mine house, do not this folly.

24 Behold, here is my daughter a maiden, and his concubine; them I will bring out now, and humble ye them, and do with them what seemeth good unto you: but unto this man do not so vile a thing.

25 But the men would not hearken to him: so the man took his concubine, and brought her forth unto them; and they knew her, and abused her all the night until the morning: and when the day began to spring, they let her go.

26 Then came the woman in the dawning of the day, and fell down at the door of the man's house where her lord was, till it was light.

27 And her lord rose up in the morning, and opened the doors of the house, and went out to go his way: and, behold, the woman his concubine was fallen down at the door of the house, and her hands were upon the threshold.

^{28} *And he said unto her, Up, and let us be going. But none answered. Then the man took her up upon an ass, and the man rose up, and gat him unto his place.*

^{29} **And when he was come into his house, he took a knife, and laid hold on his concubine, and divided her, together with her bones, into twelve pieces, and sent her into all the coasts of Israel.**

^{30} *And it was so, that all that saw it said, There was no such deed done nor seen from the day that the children of Israel came up out of the land of Egypt unto this day: consider of it, take advice, and speak your minds.*

&

Numbers 31:6-31 KJV

^{6} *And Moses sent them to the war, a thousand of every tribe, them and Phinehas the son of Eleazar the priest, to the war, with the holy instruments, and the trumpets to blow in his hand.*

^{7} *And they warred against the Midianites, as the Lord commanded Moses; and they slew all the males.*

^{8} *And they slew the kings of Midian, beside the rest of them that were slain; namely, Evi, and Rekem, and Zur, and Hur, and Reba, five kings of Midian: Balaam also the son of Beor they slew with the sword.*

^{9} *And the children of Israel took all the women of Midian captives, and their little ones, and took the spoil of all their cattle, and all their flocks, and all their goods.*

^{10} *And they burnt all their cities wherein they dwelt, and all their goodly castles, with fire.*

¹¹ And they took all the spoil, and all the prey, both of men and of beasts.

¹² And they brought the captives, and the prey, and the spoil, unto Moses, and Eleazar the priest, and unto the congregation of the children of Israel, unto the camp at the plains of Moab, which are by Jordan near Jericho.

¹³ And Moses, and Eleazar the priest, and all the princes of the congregation, went forth to meet them without the camp.

¹⁴ And Moses was wroth with the officers of the host, with the captains over thousands, and captains over hundreds, which came from the battle.

¹⁵ And Moses said unto them, Have ye saved all the women alive?

¹⁶ Behold, these caused the children of Israel, through the counsel of Balaam, to commit trespass against the Lord in the matter of Peor, and there was a plague among the congregation of the Lord.

¹⁷ Now therefore kill every male among the little ones, and kill every woman that hath known man by lying with him.

¹⁸ But all the women children, that have not known a man by lying with him, keep alive for yourselves.

¹⁹ And do ye abide without the camp seven days: whosoever hath killed any person, and whosoever hath touched any slain, purify both yourselves and your captives on the third day, and on the seventh day.

²⁰ And purify all your raiment, and all that is made of skins, and all work of goats' hair, and all things made of wood.

21 And Eleazar the priest said unto the men of war which went to the battle, This is the ordinance of the law which the Lord commanded Moses;

22 Only the gold, and the silver, the brass, the iron, the tin, and the lead,

23 Every thing that may abide the fire, ye shall make it go through the fire, and it shall be clean: nevertheless it shall be purified with the water of separation: and all that abideth not the fire ye shall make go through the water.

24 And ye shall wash your clothes on the seventh day, and ye shall be clean, and afterward ye shall come into the camp.

25 And the Lord spake unto Moses, saying,

26 Take the sum of the prey that was taken, both of man and of beast, thou, and Eleazar the priest, and the chief fathers of the congregation:

27 And divide the prey into two parts; between them that took the war upon them, who went out to battle, and between all the congregation:

28 And levy a tribute unto the Lord of the men of war which went out to battle: one soul of five hundred, both of the persons, and of the beeves, and of the asses, and of the sheep:

29 Take it of their half, and give it unto Eleazar the priest, for an heave offering of the Lord.

30 And of the children of Israel's half, thou shalt take one portion of fifty, of the persons, of the beeves, of the asses, and of the flocks, of all manner of beasts, and give them unto the Levites, which keep the charge of the tabernacle of the Lord.

31 And Moses and Eleazar the priest did as the Lord commanded Moses.

&

2 Peter 2:1 - 10 KJV

2 But there were false prophets also among the people, even as there shall be false teachers among you, who privily shall bring in damnable heresies, even denying the Lord that bought them, and bring upon themselves swift destruction.

2 And many shall follow their pernicious ways; by reason of whom the way of truth shall be evil spoken of.

3 And through covetousness shall they with feigned words make merchandise of you: whose judgment now of a long time lingereth not, and their damnation slumbereth not.

4 For if God spared not the angels that sinned, but cast them down to hell, and delivered them into chains of darkness, to be reserved unto judgment;

5 And spared not the old world, but saved Noah the eighth person, a preacher of righteousness, bringing in the flood upon the world of the ungodly;

6 And turning the cities of Sodom and Gomorrha into ashes condemned them with an overthrow, making them an ensample unto those that after should live ungodly;

7 And delivered just Lot, vexed with the filthy conversation of the wicked:

8 (For that righteous man dwelling among them, in seeing and hearing, vexed his righteous soul from day to day with their unlawful deeds;)

9 The Lord knoweth how to deliver the godly out of temptations, and to reserve the unjust unto the day of judgment to be punished:

10 But chiefly them that walk after the flesh in the lust of uncleanness, and despise government. Presumptuous are they, selfwilled, they are not afraid to speak evil of dignities.

&

Deuteronomy 22: 1-30 KJV

22 Thou shalt not see thy brother's ox or his sheep go astray, and hide thyself from them: thou shalt in any case bring them again unto thy brother.

2 And if thy brother be not nigh unto thee, or if thou know him not, then thou shalt bring it unto thine own house, and it shall be with thee until thy brother seek after it, and thou shalt restore it to him again.

3 In like manner shalt thou do with his ass; and so shalt thou do with his raiment; and with all lost thing of thy brother's, which he hath lost, and thou hast found, shalt thou do likewise: thou mayest not hide thyself.

4 Thou shalt not see thy brother's ass or his ox fall down by the way, and hide thyself from them: thou shalt surely help him to lift them up again.

5 The woman shall not wear that which pertaineth unto a man, neither shall a man put on a woman's garment: for all that do so are abomination unto the Lord thy God.

⁶ If a bird's nest chance to be before thee in the way in any tree, or on the ground, whether they be young ones, or eggs, and the dam sitting upon the young, or upon the eggs, thou shalt not take the dam with the young:

⁷ But thou shalt in any wise let the dam go, and take the young to thee; that it may be well with thee, and that thou mayest prolong thy days.

⁸ When thou buildest a new house, then thou shalt make a battlement for thy roof, that thou bring not blood upon thine house, if any man fall from thence.

⁹ Thou shalt not sow thy vineyard with divers seeds: lest the fruit of thy seed which thou hast sown, and the fruit of thy vineyard, be defiled.

¹⁰ Thou shalt not plow with an ox and an ass together.

¹¹ Thou shalt not wear a garment of divers sorts, as of woollen and linen together.

¹² Thou shalt make thee fringes upon the four quarters of thy vesture, wherewith thou coverest thyself.

¹³ If any man take a wife, and go in unto her, and hate her,

¹⁴ And give occasions of speech against her, and bring up an evil name upon her, and say, I took this woman, and when I came to her, I found her not a maid:

¹⁵ Then shall the father of the damsel, and her mother, take and bring forth the tokens of the damsel's virginity unto the elders of the city in the gate:

16 And the damsel's father shall say unto the elders, I gave my daughter unto this man to wife, and he hateth her;

17 And, lo, he hath given occasions of speech against her, saying, I found not thy daughter a maid; and yet these are the tokens of my daughter's virginity. And they shall spread the cloth before the elders of the city.

18 And the elders of that city shall take that man and chastise him;

19 And they shall amerce him in an hundred shekels of silver, and give them unto the father of the damsel, because he hath brought up an evil name upon a virgin of Israel: and she shall be his wife; he may not put her away all his days.

20 But if this thing be true, and the tokens of virginity be not found for the damsel:

21 Then they shall bring out the damsel to the door of her father's house, and the men of her city shall stone her with stones that she die: because she hath wrought folly in Israel, to play the whore in her father's house: so shalt thou put evil away from among you.

22 If a man be found lying with a woman married to an husband, then they shall both of them die, both the man that lay with the woman, and the woman: so shalt thou put away evil from Israel.

23 If a damsel that is a virgin be betrothed unto an husband, and a man find her in the city, and lie with her;

24 Then ye shall bring them both out unto the gate of that city, and ye shall stone them with stones that they die; the damsel, because she cried not, being in the city; and the man, because he hath humbled his neighbour's wife: so thou shalt put away evil from among you.

^{25} *But if a man find a betrothed damsel in the field, and the man force her, and lie with her: then the man only that lay with her shall die.*

^{26} *But unto the damsel thou shalt do nothing; there is in the damsel no sin worthy of death: for as when a man riseth against his neighbour, and slayeth him, even so is this matter:*

^{27} *For he found her in the field, and the betrothed damsel cried, and there was none to save her.*

^{28} **If a man find a damsel that is a virgin, which is not betrothed, and lay hold on her, and lie with her, and they be found;**

^{29} **Then the man that lay with her shall give unto the damsel's father fifty shekels of silver, and she shall be his wife; because he hath humbled her, he may not put her away all his days.**

^{30} *A man shall not take his father's wife, nor discover his father's skirt.*

Threatening that if people disobey him or worship other gods, he will force them to eat their own children? (Jeremiah 19:9, Leviticus 26:27-29)

Jeremiah 19:3 - 15 KJV

³ And say, Hear ye the word of the Lord, O kings of Judah, and inhabitants of Jerusalem; Thus saith the Lord of hosts, the God of Israel; Behold, I will bring evil upon this place, the which whosoever heareth, his ears shall tingle.

⁴ Because they have forsaken me, and have estranged this place, and have burned incense in it unto other gods, whom neither they nor their fathers have known, nor the kings of Judah, and have filled this place with the blood of innocents;

⁵ They have built also the high places of Baal, to burn their sons with fire for burnt offerings unto Baal, which I commanded not, nor spake it, neither came it into my mind:

⁶ Therefore, behold, the days come, saith the Lord, that this place shall no more be called Tophet, nor The valley of the son of Hinnom, but The valley of slaughter.

⁷ And I will make void the counsel of Judah and Jerusalem in this place; and I will cause them to fall by the sword before their enemies, and by the hands of them that seek their lives: and their carcases will I give to be meat for the fowls of the heaven, and for the beasts of the earth.

⁸ And I will make this city desolate, and an hissing; every one that passeth thereby shall be astonished and hiss because of all the plagues thereof.

⁹ And I will cause them to eat the flesh of their sons and the flesh of their daughters, and they shall eat every one the flesh of his

friend in the siege and straitness, wherewith their enemies, and they that seek their lives, shall straiten them.

[10] *Then shalt thou break the bottle in the sight of the men that go with thee,*

[11] *And shalt say unto them, Thus saith the Lord of hosts; Even so will I break this people and this city, as one breaketh a potter's vessel, that cannot be made whole again: and they shall bury them in Tophet, till there be no place to bury.*

[12] *Thus will I do unto this place, saith the Lord, and to the inhabitants thereof, and even make this city as Tophet:*

[13] *And the houses of Jerusalem, and the houses of the kings of Judah, shall be defiled as the place of Tophet, because of all the houses upon whose roofs they have burned incense unto all the host of heaven, and have poured out drink offerings unto other gods.*

[14] *Then came Jeremiah from Tophet, whither the Lord had sent him to prophesy; and he stood in the court of the Lord's house; and said to all the people,*

[15] *Thus saith the Lord of hosts, the God of Israel; Behold, I will bring upon this city and upon all her towns all the evil that I have pronounced against it, because they have hardened their necks, that they might not hear my words.*

&

Leviticus 26 KJV

26 Ye shall make you no idols nor graven image, neither rear you up a standing image, neither shall ye set up any image of stone in your land, to bow down unto it: for I am the Lord your God.

² Ye shall keep my sabbaths, and reverence my sanctuary: I am the Lord.

³ If ye walk in my statutes, and keep my commandments, and do them;

⁴ Then I will give you rain in due season, and the land shall yield her increase, and the trees of the field shall yield their fruit.

⁵ And your threshing shall reach unto the vintage, and the vintage shall reach unto the sowing time: and ye shall eat your bread to the full, and dwell in your land safely.

⁶ And I will give peace in the land, and ye shall lie down, and none shall make you afraid: and I will rid evil beasts out of the land, neither shall the sword go through your land.

⁷ And ye shall chase your enemies, and they shall fall before you by the sword.

⁸ And five of you shall chase an hundred, and an hundred of you shall put ten thousand to flight: and your enemies shall fall before you by the sword.

⁹ For I will have respect unto you, and make you fruitful, and multiply you, and establish my covenant with you.

¹⁰ And ye shall eat old store, and bring forth the old because of the new.

¹¹ And I set my tabernacle among you: and my soul shall not abhor you.

¹² And I will walk among you, and will be your God, and ye shall be my people.

[13] I am the Lord your God, which brought you forth out of the land of Egypt, that ye should not be their bondmen; and I have broken the bands of your yoke, and made you go upright.

[14] But if ye will not hearken unto me, and will not do all these commandments;

[15] And if ye shall despise my statutes, or if your soul abhor my judgments, so that ye will not do all my commandments, but that ye break my covenant:

[16] I also will do this unto you; I will even appoint over you terror, consumption, and the burning ague, that shall consume the eyes, and cause sorrow of heart: and ye shall sow your seed in vain, for your enemies shall eat it.

[17] And I will set my face against you, and ye shall be slain before your enemies: they that hate you shall reign over you; and ye shall flee when none pursueth you.

[18] And if ye will not yet for all this hearken unto me, then I will punish you seven times more for your sins.

[19] And I will break the pride of your power; and I will make your heaven as iron, and your earth as brass:

[20] And your strength shall be spent in vain: for your land shall not yield her increase, neither shall the trees of the land yield their fruits.

[21] And if ye walk contrary unto me, and will not hearken unto me; I will bring seven times more plagues upon you according to your sins.

²² I will also send wild beasts among you, which shall rob you of your children, and destroy your cattle, and make you few in number; and your high ways shall be desolate.

²³ And if ye will not be reformed by me by these things, but will walk contrary unto me;

²⁴ Then will I also walk contrary unto you, and will punish you yet seven times for your sins.

²⁵ And I will bring a sword upon you, that shall avenge the quarrel of my covenant: and when ye are gathered together within your cities, I will send the pestilence among you; and ye shall be delivered into the hand of the enemy.

²⁶ And when I have broken the staff of your bread, ten women shall bake your bread in one oven, and they shall deliver you your bread again by weight: and ye shall eat, and not be satisfied.

²⁷ And if ye will not for all this hearken unto me, but walk contrary unto me;

²⁸ Then I will walk contrary unto you also in fury; and I, even I, will chastise you seven times for your sins.

²⁹ And ye shall eat the flesh of your sons, and the flesh of your daughters shall ye eat.

³⁰ And I will destroy your high places, and cut down your images, and cast your carcases upon the carcases of your idols, and my soul shall abhor you.

³¹ And I will make your cities waste, and bring your sanctuaries unto desolation, and I will not smell the savour of your sweet odours.

32 And I will bring the land into desolation: and your enemies which dwell therein shall be astonished at it.

33 And I will scatter you among the heathen, and will draw out a sword after you: and your land shall be desolate, and your cities waste.

34 Then shall the land enjoy her sabbaths, as long as it lieth desolate, and ye be in your enemies' land; even then shall the land rest, and enjoy her sabbaths.

35 As long as it lieth desolate it shall rest; because it did not rest in your sabbaths, when ye dwelt upon it.

36 And upon them that are left alive of you I will send a faintness into their hearts in the lands of their enemies; and the sound of a shaken leaf shall chase them; and they shall flee, as fleeing from a sword; and they shall fall when none pursueth.

37 And they shall fall one upon another, as it were before a sword, when none pursueth: and ye shall have no power to stand before your enemies.

38 And ye shall perish among the heathen, and the land of your enemies shall eat you up.

39 And they that are left of you shall pine away in their iniquity in your enemies' lands; and also in the iniquities of their fathers shall they pine away with them.

40 If they shall confess their iniquity, and the iniquity of their fathers, with their trespass which they trespassed against me, and that also they have walked contrary unto me;

41 And that I also have walked contrary unto them, and have brought them into the land of their enemies; if then their uncircumcised hearts be humbled, and they then accept of the punishment of their iniquity:

⁴² Then will I remember my covenant with Jacob, and also my covenant with Isaac, and also my covenant with Abraham will I remember; and I will remember the land.

⁴³ The land also shall be left of them, and shall enjoy her sabbaths, while she lieth desolate without them: and they shall accept of the punishment of their iniquity: because, even because they despised my judgments, and because their soul abhorred my statutes.

⁴⁴ And yet for all that, when they be in the land of their enemies, I will not cast them away, neither will I abhor them, to destroy them utterly, and to break my covenant with them: for I am the Lord their God.

⁴⁵ But I will for their sakes remember the covenant of their ancestors, whom I brought forth out of the land of Egypt in the sight of the heathen, that I might be their God: I am the Lord.

⁴⁶ These are the statutes and judgments and laws, which the Lord made between him and the children of Israel in mount Sinai by the hand of Moses.

Exodus 10:1 KJV

10 And the Lord said unto Moses, Go in unto Pharaoh: for I have hardened his heart, and the heart of his servants, that I might shew these my signs before him:

&

Hebrews 10: 1-17 KJV

10 For the law having a shadow of good things to come, and not the very image of the things, can never with those sacrifices which they offered year by year continually make the comers thereunto perfect.

² For then would they not have ceased to be offered? because that the worshippers once purged should have had no more conscience of sins.

³ But in those sacrifices there is a remembrance again made of sins every year.

⁴ For it is not possible that the blood of bulls and of goats should take away sins.

⁵ Wherefore when he cometh into the world, he saith, Sacrifice and offering thou wouldest not, but a body hast thou prepared me:

⁶ In burnt offerings and sacrifices for sin thou hast had no pleasure.

⁷ Then said I, Lo, I come (in the volume of the book it is written of me,) to do thy will, O God.

⁸ Above when he said, Sacrifice and offering and burnt offerings and offering for sin thou wouldest not, neither hadst pleasure therein; which are offered by the law;

⁹ Then said he, Lo, I come to do thy will, O God. He taketh away the first, that he may establish the second.

¹⁰ By the which will we are sanctified through the offering of the body of Jesus Christ once for all.

¹¹ And every priest standeth daily ministering and offering oftentimes the same sacrifices, which can never take away sins:

¹² But this man, after he had offered one sacrifice for sins for ever, sat down on the right hand of God;

¹³ From henceforth expecting till his enemies be made his footstool.

¹⁴ For by one offering he hath perfected for ever them that are sanctified.

¹⁵ Whereof the Holy Ghost also is a witness to us: for after that he had said before,

¹⁶ This is the covenant that I will make with them after those days, saith the Lord, I will put my laws into their hearts, and in their minds will I write them;

¹⁷ And their sins and iniquities will I remember no more.

&

<u>1 Peter 5 King James Version</u>

5 The elders which are among you I exhort, who am also an elder, and a witness of the sufferings of Christ, and also a partaker of the glory that shall be revealed:

² Feed the flock of God which is among you, taking the oversight thereof, not by constraint, but willingly; not for filthy lucre, but of a ready mind;

³ Neither as being lords over God's heritage, but being examples to the flock.

⁴ And when the chief Shepherd shall appear, ye shall receive a crown of glory that fadeth not away.

⁵ Likewise, ye younger, submit yourselves unto the elder. Yea, all of you be subject one to another, and be clothed with humility: for God resisteth the proud, and giveth grace to the humble.

⁶ Humble yourselves therefore under the mighty hand of God, that he may exalt you in due time:

⁷ Casting all your care upon him; for he careth for you.

⁸ Be sober, be vigilant; because your adversary the devil, as a roaring lion, walketh about, seeking whom he may devour:

⁹ Whom resist stedfast in the faith, knowing that the same afflictions are accomplished in your brethren that are in the world.

¹⁰ But the God of all grace, who hath called us unto his eternal glory by Christ Jesus, after that ye have suffered a while, make you perfect, stablish, strengthen, settle you.

¹¹ To him be glory and dominion for ever and ever. Amen.

Lying, and making other people lie? (Genesis 22:2, Genesis 8:21, 2Peter 3:10-11[contradicting god's promise in Gen. 8:21, to never again destroy the Earth], Ezekiel 14:9[Where god deliberately deceives a prophet], 1Kings 22:23, 2Thessalonians 2:11)

Genesis 8:21 King James Version

²¹ And the Lord smelled a sweet savour; and the Lord said in his heart, I will not again curse the ground any more for man's sake; for the imagination of man's heart is evil from his youth; neither will I again smite any more every thing living, as I have done.

&

Genesis 22:2 KJV

² And he said, Take now thy son, thine only son Isaac, whom thou lovest, and get thee into the land of Moriah; and offer him there for a burnt offering upon one of the mountains which I will tell thee of.

&

2 Peter 3:10-11 KJV

¹⁰ But the day of the Lord will come as a thief in the night; in the which the heavens shall pass away with a great noise, and the elements shall melt with fervent heat, the earth also and the works that are therein shall be burned up.

¹¹ Seeing then that all these things shall be dissolved, what manner of persons ought ye to be in all holy conversation and godliness,

&

Ezekiel 14:9 King James Version

⁹ And if the prophet be deceived when he hath spoken a thing, I the Lord have deceived that prophet, and I will stretch out my hand upon him, and will destroy him from the midst of my people Israel.

&

1 Kings 22:23 King James Version

²³ Now therefore, behold, the Lord hath put a lying spirit in the mouth of all these thy prophets, and the Lord hath spoken evil concerning thee.

&

2 Thessalonians 2:11 King James Version

¹¹ And for this cause God shall send them strong delusion, that they should believe a lie:

Jesus Christ encourages you to hate your own family so that you

obey him. The behavior of a typical con-artist cult leader:

Luke 14:26-33 King James Version (KJV)

If any man come to me, and hate not his father, and mother, and wife, and
children, and brethren, and sisters, yea, and his own life also, he cannot be my disciple.
And whosoever doth not bear his cross, and come after me, cannot be my disciple.
For which of you, intending to build a tower, sitteth not down first, and counteth
the cost, whether he have sufficient to finish it?
Lest haply, after he hath laid the foundation, and is not able to finish it, all that
behold it begin to mock him,
Saying, This man began to build, and was not able to finish.
Or what king, going to make war against another king, sitteth not down first, and
consulteth whether he be able with ten thousand to meet him that cometh against
him with twenty thousand?
Or else, while the other is yet a great way off, he sendeth an ambassage, and
desireth conditions of peace.
So likewise, whosoever he be of you that forsaketh not all that he hath, he cannot be my disciple.

&

Jesus Christ was an Anti-Semite. After losing the debate to a

group of Jews, he says they're the children of the devil:

John 8:21-44 King James Version (KJV)

21 Then said Jesus again unto them, I go my way, and ye shall seek me, and shall die in your sins: whither I go, ye cannot come.
22 Then said the Jews, Will he kill himself? because he saith, Whither I go, ye cannot come.
23 And he said unto them, Ye are from beneath; I am from above: ye are of this world; I am not of this world.
24 I said therefore unto you, that ye shall die in your sins: for if ye believe not that I am he, ye shall die in your sins.
25 Then said they unto him, Who art thou? And Jesus saith unto them, Even the same that I said unto you from the beginning.
26 I have many things to say and to judge of you: but he that sent me is true; and I speak to the world those things which I have heard of him.
27 They understood not that he spake to them of the Father.
28 Then said Jesus unto them, When ye have lifted up the Son of man, then shall ye know that I am he, and that I do nothing of myself; but as my Father hath taught me, I speak these things.
29 And he that sent me is with me: the Father hath not left me alone; for I do always those things that please him.
30 As he spake these words, many believed on him.
31 Then said Jesus to those Jews which believed on him, If ye continue in my word, then are ye my disciples indeed;
32 And ye shall know the truth, and the truth shall make you free.
33 They answered him, We be Abraham's seed, and were never in bondage to any man: how sayest thou, Ye shall be made free?
34 Jesus answered them, Verily, verily, I say unto you, Whosoever committeth sin is the servant of sin.
35 And the servant abideth not in the house for ever: but the Son abideth ever.
36 If the Son therefore shall make you free, ye shall be free indeed.

37 I know that ye are Abraham's seed; but ye seek to kill me, because my word hath no place in you.

38 I speak that which I have seen with my Father: and ye do that which ye have seen with your father.

39 They answered and said unto him, Abraham is our father. Jesus saith unto them, If ye were Abraham's children, ye would do the works of Abraham.

40 But now ye seek to kill me, a man that hath told you the truth, which I have heard of God: this did not Abraham.

41 Ye do the deeds of your father. Then said they to him, We be not born of fornication; we have one Father, even God.

*42 **Jesus said unto them**, If God were your Father, ye would love me: for I proceeded forth and came from God; neither came I of myself, but he sent me.*

43 Why do ye not understand my speech? even because ye cannot hear my word.

44 Ye are of your father the devil, and the lusts of your father ye will do. He was a murderer from the beginning, and abode not in the truth, because there is no truth in him. When he speaketh a lie, he speaketh of his own: for he is a liar, and the father of it.

&

The Misogyny of Early Christians which is still practiced today by Billionaire Christian Conservatives in the US known as the Wilks Brothers and taught in their Christian denomination, The 7th Day Assembly of Yahwah. They promote this disgusting misogyny due to their faith in Jesus Christ.[14] Likewise, there are Christian

---

[14] "Static.reuters.com." Reuters, Reuters, static.reuters.com/resources/media/editorial/20150910/WilksDoctrinalPoints.pdf.

women in the West who encourage submission to the husband instead of equality between genders and there are Christian men who seek to find young Christian women to exploit to "groom" in order to force them to follow misogynistic teachings in the Bible.[15][16] Here are the Biblical passages that encourage such misogynistic behavior and that try to teach women it is morally right to do so as Christians:

1 Corinthians 11
King James Version

11 Be ye followers of me, even as I also am of Christ.

[2] Now I praise you, brethren, that ye remember me in all things, and keep the ordinances, as I delivered them to you.

[3] But I would have you know, that the head of every man is Christ; and the head of the woman is the man; and the head of Christ is God.

[4] Every man praying or prophesying, having his head covered, dishonoureth his head.

---

[15] Alexander, Lori. "No Verses Command Husbands to Submit to Their Wives." The Transformed Wife, 9 Nov. 2020, thetransformedwife.com/no-verses-command-husbands-to-submit-to-their-wives/.

[16] "7 Steps to Grooming Your Young Christian Wife." Biblical Gender Roles, Wordpress, 29 July 2020, biblicalgenderroles.com/2020/07/16/7-steps-to-grooming-your-christian-wife/.

⁵ But every woman that prayeth or prophesieth with her head uncovered dishonoureth her head: for that is even all one as if she were shaven.

⁶ For if the woman be not covered, let her also be shorn: but if it be a shame for a woman to be shorn or shaven, let her be covered.

⁷ For a man indeed ought not to cover his head, forasmuch as he is the image and glory of God: but the woman is the glory of the man.

⁸ For the man is not of the woman: but the woman of the man.

⁹ Neither was the man created for the woman; but the woman for the man.

¹⁰ For this cause ought the woman to have power on her head because of the angels.

¹¹ Nevertheless neither is the man without the woman, neither the woman without the man, in the Lord.

¹² For as the woman is of the man, even so is the man also by the woman; but all things of God.

¹³ Judge in yourselves: is it comely that a woman pray unto God uncovered?

¹⁴ Doth not even nature itself teach you, that, if a man have long hair, it is a shame unto him?

¹⁵ But if a woman have long hair, it is a glory to her: for her hair is given her for a covering.

¹⁶ But if any man seem to be contentious, we have no such custom, neither the churches of God.

17 Now in this that I declare unto you I praise you not, that ye come together not for the better, but for the worse.

18 For first of all, when ye come together in the church, I hear that there be divisions among you; and I partly believe it.

19 For there must be also heresies among you, that they which are approved may be made manifest among you.

20 When ye come together therefore into one place, this is not to eat the Lord's supper.

21 For in eating every one taketh before other his own supper: and one is hungry, and another is drunken.

22 What? have ye not houses to eat and to drink in? or despise ye the church of God, and shame them that have not? what shall I say to you? shall I praise you in this? I praise you not.

23 For I have received of the Lord that which also I delivered unto you, that the Lord Jesus the same night in which he was betrayed took bread:

24 And when he had given thanks, he brake it, and said, Take, eat: this is my body, which is broken for you: this do in remembrance of me.

25 After the same manner also he took the cup, when he had supped, saying, this cup is the new testament in my blood: this do ye, as oft as ye drink it, in remembrance of me.

26 For as often as ye eat this bread, and drink this cup, ye do shew the Lord's death till he come.

27 Wherefore whosoever shall eat this bread, and drink this cup of the Lord, unworthily, shall be guilty of the body and blood of the Lord.

28 But let a man examine himself, and so let him eat of that bread, and drink of that cup.

29 For he that eateth and drinketh unworthily, eateth and drinketh damnation to himself, not discerning the Lord's body.

30 For this cause many are weak and sickly among you, and many sleep.

31 For if we would judge ourselves, we should not be judged.

32 But when we are judged, we are chastened of the Lord, that we should not be condemned with the world.

33 Wherefore, my brethren, when ye come together to eat, tarry one for another.

34 And if any man hunger, let him eat at home; that ye come not together unto condemnation. And the rest will I set in order when I come.

&

This particular section is renowned by Christian men and women trying to argue that it teaches equality, but a closer inspection on the full list of verses shows that women are seen as an extension of men and not as their own independent person who can think and act for herself. In effect, this heavily implies that Christian men should treat their wives as their property and not as a person

who deserves equality and human rights.

Ephesians 5
King James Version

5 Be ye therefore followers of God, as dear children;

2 And walk in love, as Christ also hath loved us, and hath given himself for us an offering and a sacrifice to God for a sweetsmelling savour.

3 But fornication, and all uncleanness, or covetousness, let it not be once named among you, as becometh saints;

4 Neither filthiness, nor foolish talking, nor jesting, which are not convenient: but rather giving of thanks.

5 For this ye know, that no whoremonger, nor unclean person, nor covetous man, who is an idolater, hath any inheritance in the kingdom of Christ and of God.

6 Let no man deceive you with vain words: for because of these things cometh the wrath of God upon the children of disobedience.

7 Be not ye therefore partakers with them.

8 For ye were sometimes darkness, but now are ye light in the Lord: walk as children of light:

9 (For the fruit of the Spirit is in all goodness and righteousness and truth;)

10 Proving what is acceptable unto the Lord.

¹¹ And have no fellowship with the unfruitful works of darkness, but rather reprove them.

¹² For it is a shame even to speak of those things which are done of them in secret.

¹³ But all things that are reproved are made manifest by the light: for whatsoever doth make manifest is light.

¹⁴ Wherefore he saith, Awake thou that sleepest, and arise from the dead, and Christ shall give thee light.

¹⁵ See then that ye walk circumspectly, not as fools, but as wise,

¹⁶ Redeeming the time, because the days are evil.

¹⁷ Wherefore be ye not unwise, but understanding what the will of the Lord is.

¹⁸ And be not drunk with wine, wherein is excess; but be filled with the Spirit;

¹⁹ Speaking to yourselves in psalms and hymns and spiritual songs, singing and making melody in your heart to the Lord;

²⁰ Giving thanks always for all things unto God and the Father in the name of our Lord Jesus Christ;

²¹ Submitting yourselves one to another in the fear of God.

²² Wives, submit yourselves unto your own husbands, as unto the Lord.

²³ For the husband is the head of the wife, even as Christ is the head of the church: and he is the saviour of the body.

24 Therefore as the church is subject unto Christ, so let the wives be to their own husbands in every thing.

25 Husbands, love your wives, even as Christ also loved the church, and gave himself for it;

26 That he might sanctify and cleanse it with the washing of water by the word,

27 That he might present it to himself a glorious church, not having spot, or wrinkle, or any such thing; but that it should be holy and without blemish.

28 So ought men to love their wives as their own bodies. He that loveth his wife loveth himself.

29 For no man ever yet hated his own flesh; but nourisheth and cherisheth it, even as the Lord the church:

30 For we are members of his body, of his flesh, and of his bones.

31 For this cause shall a man leave his father and mother, and shall be joined unto his wife, and they two shall be one flesh.

32 This is a great mystery: but I speak concerning Christ and the church.

33 Nevertheless let every one of you in particular so love his wife even as himself; and the wife see that she reverence her husband.

&

The blatant misogyny is reinforced in later New Testament passages too. They're treated analogous to slavery with the encouragement of slaves obeying masters with the passages

explaining that it is what Jesus Christ wants. I've chosen to highlight

the commanding parts to show this is indeed to reinforce the

misogynistic teachings of Jesus Christ himself:

Colossians 3
King James Version

3 If ye then be risen with Christ, seek those things which are above, where Christ sitteth on the right hand of God.

² Set your affection on things above, not on things on the earth.

³ For ye are dead, and your life is hid with Christ in God.

⁴ When Christ, who is our life, shall appear, then shall ye also appear with him in glory.

⁵ Mortify therefore your members which are upon the earth; fornication, uncleanness, inordinate affection, evil concupiscence, and covetousness, which is idolatry:

⁶ For which things' sake the wrath of God cometh on the children of disobedience:

⁷ In the which ye also walked some time, when ye lived in them.

⁸ But now ye also put off all these; anger, wrath, malice, blasphemy, filthy communication out of your mouth.

⁹ Lie not one to another, seeing that ye have put off the old man with his deeds;

¹⁰ And have put on the new man, which is renewed in knowledge after the image of him that created him:

¹¹ Where there is neither Greek nor Jew, circumcision nor uncircumcision, Barbarian, Scythian, bond nor free: but Christ is all, and in all.

¹² Put on therefore, as the elect of God, holy and beloved, bowels of mercies, kindness, humbleness of mind, meekness, longsuffering;

¹³ Forbearing one another, and forgiving one another, if any man have a quarrel against any: even as Christ forgave you, so also do ye.

¹⁴ And above all these things put on charity, which is the bond of perfectness.

¹⁵ And let the peace of God rule in your hearts, to the which also ye are called in one body; and be ye thankful.

¹⁶ Let the word of Christ dwell in you richly in all wisdom; teaching and admonishing one another in psalms and hymns and spiritual songs, singing with grace in your hearts to the Lord.

¹⁷ And whatsoever ye do in word or deed, do all in the name of the Lord Jesus, giving thanks to God and the Father by him.

*¹⁸ **Wives, submit yourselves unto your own husbands, as it is fit in the Lord.***

¹⁹ Husbands, love your wives, and be not bitter against them.

²⁰ Children, obey your parents in all things: for this is well pleasing unto the Lord.

²¹ Fathers, provoke not your children to anger, lest they be discouraged.

²² Servants, obey in all things your masters according to the flesh; not with eyeservice, as menpleasers; but in singleness of heart, fearing God;

²³ And whatsoever ye do, do it heartily, as to the Lord, and not unto men;

²⁴ Knowing that of the Lord ye shall receive the reward of the inheritance: for ye serve the Lord Christ.

²⁵ But he that doeth wrong shall receive for the wrong which he hath done: and there is no respect of persons.

&

Christian women and female Christian preachers not associated with more hard-right conservative Christianity have attempted to reorganize the context of this specific passage by arguing it was either specific to the time or specific to the activity, but those who accept precisely what it states have tried to work around this particular passage by arguing that female Christian preachers are being subservient to male authority within Churches. Thereby, Christian women are held to a lesser status for simply being women and their sole purpose in life is directed at raising

children. Not exactly promoting equality among genders, is it?

1 Timothy 2: 1-15 King James Version (KJV)

2 I exhort therefore, that, first of all, supplications, prayers, intercessions, and giving of thanks, be made for all men;

2 For kings, and for all that are in authority; that we may lead a quiet and peaceable life in all godliness and honesty.

3 For this is good and acceptable in the sight of God our Saviour;

4 Who will have all men to be saved, and to come unto the knowledge of the truth.

5 For there is one God, and one mediator between God and men, the man Christ Jesus;

6 Who gave himself a ransom for all, to be testified in due time.

7 Whereunto I am ordained a preacher, and an apostle, (I speak the truth in Christ, and lie not;) a teacher of the Gentiles in faith and verity.

8 I will therefore that men pray every where, lifting up holy hands, without wrath and doubting.

9 In like manner also, that women adorn themselves in modest apparel, with shamefacedness and sobriety; not with broided hair, or gold, or pearls, or costly array;

10 But (which becometh women professing godliness) with good works.

11 Let the woman learn in silence with all subjection.

12 But I suffer not a woman to teach, nor to usurp authority over the man, but to be in silence.

13 For Adam was first formed, then Eve.

14 And Adam was not deceived, but the woman being deceived was in the transgression.

15 Notwithstanding she shall be saved in childbearing, if they continue in faith and charity and holiness with sobriety

&

This passage from Peter encourages Christian husbands to make Christian wives submit in fear; thus, coercion and threats to one's wife is encouraged to keep a family together in Christianity's New Testament teachings:

1 Peter 3
King James Version

3 Likewise, ye wives, be in subjection to your own husbands; that, if any obey not the word, they also may without the word be won by the conversation of the wives;

2 While they behold your chaste conversation coupled with fear.

3 Whose adorning let it not be that outward adorning of plaiting the hair, and of wearing of gold, or of putting on of apparel;

4 But let it be the hidden man of the heart, in that which is not corruptible, even the ornament of a meek and quiet spirit, which is in the sight of God of great price.

5 For after this manner in the old time the holy women also, who trusted in God, adorned themselves, being in subjection unto their own husbands:

6 Even as Sara obeyed Abraham, calling him lord: whose daughters ye are, as long as ye do well, and are not afraid with any amazement.

7 Likewise, ye husbands, dwell with them according to knowledge, giving honour unto the wife, as unto the weaker vessel, and as being heirs together of the grace of life; that your prayers be not hindered.

8 Finally, be ye all of one mind, having compassion one of another, love as brethren, be pitiful, be courteous:

9 Not rendering evil for evil, or railing for railing: but contrariwise blessing; knowing that ye are thereunto called, that ye should inherit a blessing.

10 For he that will love life, and see good days, let him refrain his tongue from evil, and his lips that they speak no guile:

11 Let him eschew evil, and do good; let him seek peace, and ensue it.

12 For the eyes of the Lord are over the righteous, and his ears are open unto their prayers: but the face of the Lord is against them that do evil.

13 And who is he that will harm you, if ye be followers of that which is good?

14 But and if ye suffer for righteousness' sake, happy are ye: and be not afraid of their terror, neither be troubled;

15 But sanctify the Lord God in your hearts: and be ready always to give an answer to every man that asketh you a reason of the hope that is in you with meekness and fear:

16 Having a good conscience; that, whereas they speak evil of you, as of evildoers, they may be ashamed that falsely accuse your good conversation in Christ.

17 For it is better, if the will of God be so, that ye suffer for well doing, than for evil doing.

18 For Christ also hath once suffered for sins, the just for the unjust, that he might bring us to God, being put to death in the flesh, but quickened by the Spirit:

19 By which also he went and preached unto the spirits in prison;

20 Which sometime were disobedient, when once the longsuffering of God waited in the days of Noah, while the ark was a preparing, wherein few, that is, eight souls were saved by water.

21 The like figure whereunto even baptism doth also now save us (not the putting away of the filth of the flesh, but the answer of a good conscience toward God,) by the resurrection of Jesus Christ:

22 Who is gone into heaven, and is on the right hand of God; angels and authorities and powers being made subject unto him.

&

While seemingly innocuous, this further shows that the duty of Christian women as commanded by their God, Yahweh, is to serve in childrearing at home and then encourage younger women to such a purpose when they've become old:

Titus 2
King James Version

2 But speak thou the things which become sound doctrine:

2 That the aged men be sober, grave, temperate, sound in faith, in charity, in patience.

3 The aged women likewise, that they be in behaviour as becometh holiness, not false accusers, not given to much wine, teachers of good things;

4 That they may teach the young women to be sober, to love their husbands, to love their children,

5 To be discreet, chaste, keepers at home, good, obedient to their own husbands, that the word of God be not blasphemed.

6 Young men likewise exhort to be sober minded.

7 In all things shewing thyself a pattern of good works: in doctrine shewing uncorruptness, gravity, sincerity,

8 Sound speech, that cannot be condemned; that he that is of the contrary part may be ashamed, having no evil thing to say of you.

⁹ Exhort servants to be obedient unto their own masters, and to please them well in all things; not answering again;

¹⁰ Not purloining, but shewing all good fidelity; that they may adorn the doctrine of God our Saviour in all things.

¹¹ For the grace of God that bringeth salvation hath appeared to all men,

¹² Teaching us that, denying ungodliness and worldly lusts, we should live soberly, righteously, and godly, in this present world;

¹³ Looking for that blessed hope, and the glorious appearing of the great God and our Saviour Jesus Christ;

¹⁴ Who gave himself for us, that he might redeem us from all iniquity, and purify unto himself a peculiar people, zealous of good works.

¹⁵ These things speak, and exhort, and rebuke with all authority. Let no man despise thee.

Chapter 4: My Opinion on Evangelical Christianity and How to Prevent its Growth

I had written the next chapter's short, question-style section out of frustration with the 2015 political events in India. I can understand being annoyed and angered by Christian missionaries who proselytize and forcibly convert Hindus to Jesus Christ. However, reacting with violence or covertly supporting parties that allow violence is completely unethical and I consider it to be anti-Hindu. Hinduism, Sanatana Dharma, should always be about peace and kindness. India has a rich history of rational and skeptical thought that has been ignored by the majority of Hindus for years and I think that, if you or anyone that you know truly wish to effectively stop forced conversions and unethical practices that lead to conversions, that you must respond with skeptical inquiry towards Christianity. If you are truly passionate about stopping the spread of Christianity then it is in your best interest to use skeptical inquiry. Christianity is dying out in the US and Europe, not because of violence but because of skeptical inquiry. The Atheist movements in

Western civilization have reduced Christianity into looking childish and stupid. India has a rich argumentative tradition in skeptical inquiry and I believe that it's the only effective way to challenge these conversion tactics. Violence will only make Hinduism look evil and it is an anti-Hindu action to do. So please, consider what I have to say. The next chapter offers you a list of questions to confront or politely ask proselytizers with when you see them or to effectively stop them from their predatory tactics. You have to risk looking annoying to truly do this. This book is mostly a guide, conversations are obviously more fluid and voluminous but I hope that helping you utilize your own arguments by providing the examples in the next chapter will help to stun and confuse the Christian missionary and bring doubt to those who are viewing them or forming a crowd around them.

Evangelical Christianity is currently propagating throughout India, China, several parts of Africa, and other places because it is dying out in the West. Christianity has lost its stronghold in the Western world and the majority of Westerners are "Christian" in name only. The only time they really practice faith, at least in the US, is when they circumcise their child and have funerals for their family. Buddhism is slowly overtaking the US and Islam is slowly overtaking Europe. Evangelical preachers are scared so they, and their many British and American corporate backers, have funded and backed Christian missionary efforts in India to convert the majority of the rural and uneducated population because they see them as easy pickings. I'll be blunt, if you truly wish to stop Christian missionaries, then Hindus need to set-up social support systems and institutions of their own to effectively help people with food, money, and housing or you can expect Christianity to be the majority religion in the years to come. Hindus are down to 79% as of the last data percentages on the number of self-described Hindus in India according to the 2011 survey by the Indian government. What makes it easy is the negative attitudes towards Dalits, which I'm sure missionaries take advantage of. If you truly wish to stop these conversion practices, then you'll need to effectively challenge these groups where they proselytize; in market places, outside shops, and especially in rural areas. Although, in the case of rural areas – and their possible danger – you should use a buddy system where you go in groups. I think simply providing food, money, or building requirements to make a house would be a better alternative. That may sound foolish, but it's the chief reason that conversions to Christianity are happening. People need help and are being ignored. What choice do they have? What options does the majority of the Hindu population leave them with? Make no mistake, there are starving children to consider and poverty needs to diminish for India to truly get out of the current trap. People cannot just blame the current government and not do anything constructive about the social issues themselves. Obviously, all necessary precautions regarding diseases like COVID-19 must be taken into account as well.

Regardless, I hope these arguments are helpful and provide you with some aid in dealing with the growing concern of forced and coercive conversions of innocent Hindus. I shall provide some social context for the questions and links to certain unsavory aspects of

Christianity so that you can formulate your own questions but they're linked to websites that can only be read in American English. The objective of these questions is to discredit the Christian missionary and Christianity. That can only be done through systematic inquiry and skepticism. Blasphemy laws, enacting stricter laws on their practices, and complaining to the government aren't going to do much when very few people pay taxes to the civic institutions in India and when police and courts are bogged down due to the lack of Judges and infrastructure; that will not help matters. That needs to be ameliorated for law enforcement to be more effective in stopping and criminalizing these incidents, but even then, it makes Christians look like martyrs which are what they want. Violence upon them is completely stupid and would only illicit sympathy for Christianity and enhances their arguments about Hinduism being devil worship – which is what they secretly think about Hinduism and what they want to expunge for the sake of their narcissistic god. They see Hinduism as evil because of the tenants of their faith about worshipping so-called "False idols" that they perceive to be devil worship. Skeptical inquiry will do far more and is by far a more peaceful tactic than violence.

If you wish to use these lines of questioning, then I recommend writing them down, using small cards to record them, printing them and sharing them among friends or passionate Hindus, and using them to form your own questions. Writing them down can also be of help for memorization and to provide as examples to others who are interested. The point is to make the crowd or people that Christian missionaries are looking to convert into observing these weaknesses in conversation and doubting Christianity's goodness. However, please be sure to maintain civility and politely inquire when you see these people proselytizing so that they're interested in your questions. Always remember, questioning them on their faith hurts them worse than violence ever will. Violence makes their convictions stronger and makes them feel justified in whatever barbaric practices they commit. Questioning Christianity is far more effective, because nearly all Evangelical Christians privately recognize the inaccuracies of their religious faith to the world that they live in. On the outset, they show solidarity and try to gain more converts to make themselves believe in their faith more strongly. By making the missionary question their religious beliefs, you are doing more harm and shaking the very core of their personhood. They secretly know the inconsistencies and try to gain more converts to believe in the religion more strongly. By making them question their faith, it increases their private doubts.

I don't know how good this book has been for you, but I hope that it helps do some good in stopping the conversions to one of the most violent religions ever created by humankind. Please consider what I've written in this book, and perhaps form your own questions using this as groundwork. I hope this one small attempt has been helpful.

Understanding Evangelical Christianity

I will briefly give my opinions about Christianity and in particular Evangelical Christianity and why they do what they do. Please read and consider this insight so that you may be able to more effectively respond to these Christian missionaries and stop them.

Christians believe that they need to convert everyone in the world to Christianity so that Christians can be flown away to heaven after Israel is attacked and destroyed by some evil demonic force made by Satan. They think that once Israel is destroyed then the end of the world will commence. They believe that all non-Christians are "doomed" to suffer on earth while Jesus saves his chosen to send them to heaven after fighting Satan and the Anti-Christ in a massive world war. They believe Jesus defeats the Anti-Christ in a final battle and Christians are then "raptured" to a new world with Jesus Christ to live eternally. This belief is the true motivator behind their conversions and it is where you must question the missionaries most on this issue. By forcing them to feel ashamed or significantly less confident, it will shake their beliefs.

Physical harm upon them only strengthens their belief, they enjoy feeling persecuted and harmed. It makes them feel as if they've succeeded in showing that they're better than Hindus, Muslims,

Buddhists, and Sikhs. It means they don't have to think about their faith at all and thus ignore their doubts. They view all non-Christian faiths, including Judaism, as devil worship and truly believe they're doing God's work. They are self-deluded, insane, and unwilling to compromise and showing them reasons to doubt their faith is the only way to effectively stop them because it confuses their beliefs. They will stop at nothing to destroy India's rich culture, commit cultural genocide, and the genocides they did to the Native Americans, Africa, the Celtics, and what they're currently doing to Thailand are irrefutable proof of this history and its current impacts; but they can be peacefully stopped despite their insanity. The Goa Inquisition is the truth of Christianity's natural interaction with the rest of the world. They have successfully committed genocide and destroyed the cultures of Tasmanian aboriginals, several African cultures, the Native Americans (who they refer to as "Indian"), and they wish for endless war with Muslims and Islam because they view Islam as the worst form of devil worship. They have done all of this through superior military force back when the West was the dominant power for 500 years. Unfortunately, I am not making up their insane desire to war endlessly with Islam, several US weapons industries manufacture weapons to use for bombing campaigns upon Muslims throughout the Middle East, Afghanistan, and Pakistan. I shall provide a youtube link in the sources to show what 50 million of these people in the US honestly believe is their religious duty to make war with Islam. To that end, they try to make Hindus and Muslims in India hate each other so they can decry both as devil worship to convert both to Christianity. The proud Christian British during their rule used a political theory called the Realist theory of International Relations to worsen the divide between Hindus and Muslim Indians by either forced starvation, placing them in the most deplorable work camps that caused massive diseases to spread, refused to sell grain to Indians who were starving, allowed massive illiteracy and poverty to go unchecked, and justified it all not just through the Realist theory of International Relations. The Christian British justify it to themselves through their belief in original sin and the fact Jesus forgives Christians of whatever crime they commit upon others. Be it lying, theft, murder, rape, or genocide; Jesus Christ forgives Christians of all crimes. That is the fundamental belief in Christianity. That is why the West can continue committing massive bombing campaigns in Afghanistan and Pakistan and simply ask Jesus to forgive them of their crimes. Many Christians, especially the Evangelicals, also see endless war with Islam as a duty. They can never say it outright, because it is a crazy belief, but Evangelical Christians strongly believe that Hinduism and especially Islam need to be wiped out through any means necessary. Some use charities and kindness, others use violence and forced conversions.

The Evangelical Christians despise anything different from them and view different beliefs as blasphemy. They hate anything that is different from Jesus Christ. They are unrepentant in their murder, rape, and genocides. They take joy in being persecuted, beaten, harassed, and murdered because they believe they're going to heaven for it. The Christian extremist enjoys death more than anyone enjoys life. That is what a true Evangelical Christianity is – a death cult. Evangelical Christianity is a fundamental hatred for all human life; a desire for world genocide so that Jesus sends them to another world of "perfection" with Jesus as ruler. Evangelical Christianity is truly the worst blight upon the world that seeks to force everyone to submit to await a mass Holocaust of innocent Jewish people and then an even more massive genocide of the world. That is the true core of Christianity and especially Evangelical Christianity.

It may sound insane to request only peaceful criticism as a means of defense, but what you need to understand is that it does far more damage than violence. Evangelical Christians behave that way because they don't want to question their religion and want to show they have no doubts about it in order to prove to others and themselves that their faith is sincere. Please, don't hate them. Be true to the peaceful nature of whatever religion that you believe and recognize what a sorry state that these people are in. Evangelical Christians may act happy and charming to you, but what they fundamentally desire is their own suicide. That is why they enjoy the thought of being killed by people of other religious faiths, they hate their lives so much that being killed by others is seen as a joy because it gives what little meaning that they view their own lives into their strange idea of maximizing their own importance for something they self-delude themselves into believing is greater than them. That is also why they do so many unsavory practices to convert people; they hate their lives so much that they wish others to experience the same pain as them. They believe that their concessions to Jesus Christ is somehow a strength above others and makes them morally superior because they think it shows their "humility" but in reality, other religious faiths scare them because they're proof that Christianity could be wrong and they can't understand other religions because of how close-minded they are. They need to see foreigners converting so they can feel strength in their Christianity because they suffer from so much doubt and yearn for their lives to end; which is why they believe in their world mass genocide with Jesus coming down to send them to a worldly heaven. They are a pitiable, depressed, and self-hating death cult that seeks conversions to comfort and affirm their own beliefs because they doubt Christianity so much in their private thoughts. They hate themselves and yearn for suicide by Christ through the idea of martyrdom.

Evangelical Christianity is not a freedom. It is the worst form of living. Not outwardly, but inwardly, it is the worst belief system imaginable. In the Sermon on the Mount, Jesus Christ teaches his followers to look for hypocrisy everywhere and condemn anyone who seems to be a hypocrite to you. Evangelical Christians believe any lewd thoughts is proof of "original sin" and an insult to their God because Jesus Christ tells them that thinking of other women while having a spouse or a girlfriend is cheating on your wife or girlfriend. That is a fundamental belief in a "thought crime" – the crime of thinking outside of a certain way. It is also false. Modern psychology has found that people's thoughts simply come and go, they are not an indication of your personal desires. Thus, Christianity is perpetual mental self-torture over having "wrong" or "evil" thoughts; in other words, they're delusional and live with unrealistic expectations. In Christianity, you aren't ever free from evil and instead of being free to believe in Gods, you become a prisoner of a single god's expectations and you must constantly view yourself as sinful, only capable of evil, and seek this god's forgiveness for committing any evil upon others so that you never feel guilty of the crimes that you commit. It is no wonder that so many criminals in the first world profess to Jesus Christ and are told they will be forgiven for their crimes. If mass murders and serial rapists can be forgiven through Jesus Christ, then how is he a good moral teacher and how is this religion not simply recognized as a criminal organization? All you have to do is seek Christ's forgiveness for the crime of your existence to forgive yourself of any crime that you commit upon innocent people. I genuinely don't know what else to say about the structure of this belief system except to say that it's insanity given a systematized structure. I am not even trying to be insulting, I genuinely tried to keep an objective and impartial view of this religious belief but the more I learned, and the more stories of forced conversions that I read about, the more I grew concerned about just what these people are actually capable of doing to innocent Hindus, innocent Muslims, innocent Sikhs, innocent Jews, innocent Buddhists, innocent Zoroastrianists, and other innocents in India.

The only true way to fight against these predatory conversion practices and even forced conversion is to make them question their own beliefs. Violence will never work; rational thought and the argumentative tradition of India will be the only true weapon against these beliefs. That is why they are predatory and aim for the poor, because the West has questioned and shown how weak their beliefs are. If India wishes to become a first world country in the coming years, then it must realign with the path of ancient India's rich history of skeptical inquiry and multicultural tolerance for questioning people's beliefs and discussing them. The traditions practiced or tolerated by Buddha, Ashoka, Akbar, every Vedic Darshana that uses the Pramana logic system, and the Charvaka philosophy. If any of these sounds controversial, they shouldn't. In their own way, each of these people or philosophies expanded free thought and freedom of expression. We Indians should be proud of our rich cultural heritage and try to educate our population to bring forth a better world for ourselves and our fellow Indians. Evangelical

Christians, in reality, are in deep depression and doubt about their

faith, and bringing forth their doubts will weaken their resolve and

make them seriously question their own methods. If you think this is

silly, just look at all of their discussions in the West. It has decreased

their numbers and made them look evil to the majority of the

Western societies. Skeptical inquiry is the only peaceful, rational,

and pro-active way to stop these forced conversions. I suggest

making a group of people with at least one person having a recording

device and questioning these Christian extremists on their beliefs. If

they become violent with you, then you have the recording device

and you can then upload to online video websites to show the true

actions of these people. Don't give up. If you wish to protect Indian

culture from their cultural genocide, then you must either donate to

the poor in India so they can live in a better standard of living and

make skeptical inquiries to these Christian missionaries. Who will

stop the Christian conversions in India by predatory Christian

missionaries? The Indian people must work together to accomplish this peacefully and rationally by themselves. I have written the next chapter to help you do that. I honestly don't know what success you may have but I hope this book is of help to you. I wish you all the best of luck in protecting Indian culture, a rich culture that is being attacked by Christian missionaries' predatory practices.

Chapter 5: Examples of Questions to Ask Christian Missionaries

The questions in this chapter can be utilized via framing the argument. These are just examples to help you formulate your own questions. Psychologists have found that you can motivate people into conducting actions or affirming stricter beliefs by framing seemingly innocent questions to affirm their commitment to a particular belief and then raise less savory questions to make them feel committed to that specific belief; because they have felt committed to the initial question, they will affirm their support for the next set of questions to stay consistent with their beliefs even if what they're advocating for is absurd. It is because of their desire for consistency with the beliefs that they've espoused; if you're curious, then I recommend reading Influence: Science and Practice by Robert B. Cialdini for more on that. Also, humans live by a universal principle of reciprocity. If someone does a kind action for you, then you feel as if you owe them and if someone does a terrible crime to you, then you feel as if you must repay the action for the sake of fairness. Christians utilize this technique to make Hindus and Muslims war with each other to then make them believe their religions are evil and goad them into converting by impressing Hindus and Muslims with their money and extravagant wealth. They know that Hindus and Muslims group each other negatively by association bias, believing the entire group of Hindus or Muslims are collectively responsible for a scant few troublemakers and criminals. While gangs of Hindus and Muslims do commit crimes, it is important to recognize each of those groups are just violent gangs and not representative of the majority of Indians.

For anyone still asking why they should trouble themselves with this task or who believe their community's religious beliefs will never change because you've lived like that since ancient times; know that Native Americans, Tasmanians, and the Celtics all believed that too before their societies were wiped out, their Gods defaced, and their culture destroyed by Christian missionaries. Granted, Christianity had armed military force back then, but it is still true that Christianity seeks to either create or impose weaknesses to exploit in a society in order to force conversions. By emphatically telling them no through peaceful means, they lose all power. You must be the hope that you wish to see. If you still question why you should make this commitment, I can only say this: We pursue these things so that others can have what we did not.

What you must have:

•	A recording device of some kind (camcorder, camera phone, or other recording device).

•	A friend or relative to record the conversation that you have with the Christian Missionary.

•	A printer to print out some of the sources I've provided in the last chapter.

•	Internet access to post these videos online on popular video websites such as Youtube or other video websites.

•	Resolve and willingness to protect Indian culture from these predatory missionaries.

Some questions are written in sequence and others are stand-alone. For sequential questions: Start with 1, then ask question 2, and then 3. Questions such as "4A" or "4B" means you choose which you prefer will be more effective. Noticing the stand-alone and sequential differences should be obvious. This is a guidepost for skeptical inquiry; ask questions that you believe will be effective in discrediting the Christian missionaries. If you feel you're not making progress with your own questions, then you can always use these questions. Be sure to print out the "sources" and hand them out appropriately when asking specific questions. I hope this book provides value and an effective response to these predatory missionaries. I sincerely hope you are successful in your endeavors. I recommend teaching these questions and their contexts to people in rural areas or better yet, providing food and money for construction so that you prove that Hinduism is a genuinely positive force on earth and diminish the likelihood of predatory Christian missionaries taking advantage. Please seriously give my suggestions some consideration. Thank you.

Section 1: Original Sin

This line of questioning pertains to the Abrahamic concept of Original Sin. Christians believe that every human being on earth is born sinful and can only escape sin through the acceptance of Jesus Christ as their lord and savior. Remember to have someone record the conversation.

Politely introduce yourself and tell them that you have some questions.

1.) "Do you believe in Original Sin?"

If they say "Yes":

2.) "Then, do you believe that people who don't accept Jesus will murder, rape, and torture others?"

If they give an affirmative (or evasive) "Yes":

3.) "So, do you believe the majority of us Indians are murderers, rapists, and torturers? Do you believe we are capable of all that because we don't accept your God?"

If they say "No" to #1:

"Then you have no reason to believe in Jesus Christ. He wouldn't have died for anyone's sins because there is none."

If they say "No" to #2 or #3:

"Then there is no reason to believe in Jesus Christ and you have no reason to try to convert us. We're living proof that your faith is wrong. Is that why you proselytize here and not the in your own country?"

After that, ask them #4. Begin by asking them politely. Such as: "One more question, please! I'm just curious to know more about your faith."

If they act rudely, point it out to any crowd of people nearby who are watching but don't holler it across the area. Just say enough so the crowd understands that the Christian converter sees themselves as superior to Indians because they just admit that.

If they accept your next question:

4A.) "So, if I understand this correctly, your belief in Jesus Christ is the only thing stopping you from rampantly assaulting, murdering, or raping us?"

Or

4B.) "So, if I understand correctly, you believe that Jesus Christ is the only thing preventing you from assaulting, murdering, and raping your own family?"

After that, politely bid farewell and say that you find their morals to be repulsive, evil, and that they just admitted to being a psychopath who is willing to kill innocent Indian children or their own children and that Indians are living proof that Christian morality is evil. Be sure that you've copied this conversation on a camera or phone and to upload it online on popular video websites mentioning that it's about Christian conversions in India. Gaining more views for these conversations will spread more awareness of this issue and

make people pay more attention to the conversions happening in

India, thus causing political leaders to be more engaged with this

issue. Always remember to maintain politeness in your questions and

not smug superiority. Explain in your video why you asked these

questions and what concerns you about Christian conversions.

Section 2: Christian Heaven

Jesus Christ is seen as the only way to heaven by Christians. These lines of questions will be especially damning for Evangelicals because it will make them confront a rather horrible idea that they never knew before. US citizens and British citizens have grown up viewing the Holocaust as the worst genocide to ever happen. It was certainly a horrific event, but all genocides are equally as horrible as any other. These questions will force them to confront a sinister aspect of Christian theology that they probably never considered.

1.) "Do you believe Jesus Christ is the only way to heaven?"

2.) "So, you believe our ancestors, and the ancestors of Christian Indians, are all in hell?"

3.) "Do you believe that the Jews who died in the Holocaust are also in hell?"

If they say "No", try to evade or backtrack, or try to ignore question #1:

"So people can go to heaven without believing in Jesus Christ as their lord and savior? Then nobody needs Christianity."

If they say "No" or continue to try to evade questions #2 and #3:

"Well, it looks like your religion can't handle a few basic questions. Maybe you should think more about your faith because it doesn't seem true to me and I don't think that you really believe in it. I see no reason to believe that those who died in the Holocaust are in hell or purgatory for the crime of not being Christian like you do. Such a belief seems insane and would mean more suffering for innocent Jewish people who suffered and died in one of the worst genocides in human history."

Bid farewell politely. Make sure to videotape or have someone record this conversation on a phone to upload it online on youtube and other popular and public video websites to spread the awareness of the issue and to show the weakness of Christian theology. Add your own opinions on why you think Christian theology is a failure.

Section 3: Christian rape crimes, the Holocaust, and US wars

You'll probably only be able to use one of these conversations numbered "1,2,3" respectively because they're likely to stir resentment from the missionaries but be sure to video tape these events. Have a printed copy of Source 1, Maze of Injustice, to show them. Should the Christian missionary be an American, politely introduce yourself and ask them if they are. Then ask the following:

1.) "If Christianity is peaceful, then why are there massive rapes of Native Americans in Alaska and other parts of the United States – the greatest Christian country in the world?"

If they deny or evade the question by trying to throw a question back at you:

"I'm only asking because you refer to them wrongly as Indians. Christians rape them every day in the United States and it is never talked about. Is that what you intend to do to the Indians here? Children have suffered rapes in the United States, for simply being Native American and your people constantly refer to them as Indian. Why do you refer to them as Indian and how can Christianity call itself peaceful after destroying their culture and continuing mass rapes every day?"

If they get angry or try to walk away then show them your Maze of Injustice copy.

"Sir, I'm not trying to start an argument. I just have questions! I want to know why you Christians destroyed Native American culture, rape their children, and continue to do that today? Your denial shows your inability to accept criticism."

If they ask for proof, show them the copy of Source 1, Maze of Injustice, that you have printed out and hand it to them.

"See! Christians are raping Indians to this day! Christian churches throughout the world have raped people in India too! Why do you continue to deny the problems of your religion? You proselytize that it's peaceful but you run away when confronted with the truth of Christian crimes throughout the world? That doesn't sound like a peaceful religion to me!"

Be sure to film this conversation and have an explanation for the Source material, Maze of Injustice. Explain that Christians continue to deny rape atrocities in the United States and try to make third world countries look like the only perpetrators and that you thought the Christian nations were better than third world countries but the evidence says otherwise – Christians just deny their rape crimes of people they refer to as "Indians" and you fear for your fellow Indians.

If the Christian missionaries are Jehovah's witnesses, show them a print out of source 3. If they're another denomination of Christianity then source 2.

For this next one, briefly introduce yourself and say that you were reading the news about terrorism and it made you think about Christianity.

2.) "How can you call Christianity peaceful when Christian countries always bomb Muslim countries and call themselves humanitarian for causing massive deaths?"

If they deny the accusation or ignore or evade the question:

2A.) "The greatest Christian country in the world, the United States, is bombing Yemen, Iraq, Afghanistan, Pakistan, Syria, the Philippines and who knows where else and your people call bomb droppings on innocent Muslim civilians humanitarian?"

Ask this one more loudly. You can even ask it after asking question 2A.

2B.) "Do you believe that all Muslims are going to hell because they deny Jesus Christ is the Son of God?"

If they say "Yes" to 2B then speak this loudly:

"Then how is your religion peaceful, if you condemn so many innocent Muslims to hell? How can you condemn innocent children to bomb droppings that kill innocents? Christian morals don't seem to have any sense of empathy or responsibility! You just throw all your responsibility and compassion away by telling yourself that Christ will take care of it! That is completely delusional!"

If they deny 2B or evade the question:

"Well, if you believe they're not going to hell then why are you trying to convert them and others? There would be no reason to believe in Jesus Christ and that's the reason that you're doing this. So maybe you should think more about what you're doing?"

After that, tell them their morality is self-centered and arrogant; tell them they have no humility or compassion for non-Christians because they believe that everything is evil and presuppose evil intent upon everyone through their belief in sinfulness and thus allows them to do deceitful practices that go against the commandment about lying. Tell them that they forgive themselves of any crime they do upon others through Christ and therefore have no true moral values.

If you are confronted by non-Christians about this line of questioning, just point out that you're honestly concerned with the forced conversions that Christians are trying to do on so many people and that these practices seem to be everywhere in India.

&

Christian Europe and certain parts of Christian America have a history of persecution of the Jews. By contrast,

Hindus and Jews have lived in peace and harmony for 2400 years. Christians believe that they need to convert all the Jews to Jesus Christ because they believe biblical Jewish prophecies were fulfilled by Jesus Christ. They see Jews as misguided and want them to convert to Christianity to await the end of the world so Jesus can fight the Anti-Christ as the world is destroyed.

3.) "If Christianity is the most peaceful faith, then why did Christians persecute Jews throughout Europe's history while Hindus never did for 2400 years?"

If they try to make-up a reason (it's most likely going to be bogus or a non-answer):

"Doesn't that prove that Eastern Faiths and Judaism are more peaceful than Christianity? We never persecuted or warred with our Jewish Indians and are proud of our mutual respect for 2400 years. Why should we convert to a faith that tries to force them to convert? That seems anti-Semitic."

If they deny the persecutions being part of Christianity:

"Miss/Sir! The Nazis wore the belt buckle stating 'God with Us' and the Pope at the time made Hitler's birthday a national holiday. The Holocaust was a Christian genocide of Jews. In fact, the Goa Inquisition of Catholic Christians burned down Jewish synagogues in India because they believed Jews were evil because that's what their faith in Jesus led them to believe. That proves that believing in Jesus Christ doesn't make people more peaceful. If you're trying to convert Jews and believe they have the wrong faith, then you're just the same as the Nazis! You have no respect for Jews, unlike Indians/Hindus!"

If they get angry or try to evade:

"Sir, your faith is anti-Semitic because you believe Israel needs to be destroyed so that Jesus can fight the Anti-Christ after some mass world genocide of Jews. Your bible says Jews will be sent to hell to be judged by Satan in Revelations. So you want a bigger Holocaust than Hitler so that you can go to heaven! That's evil and selfish!"

If they get angry, leave, or deny your accusations:

"Miss/Sir! You're proving how little faith you have by running away! It seems you cannot confront the evil of Jewish persecution in your religious faith and so try to preach to others through dishonest means! Your religion isn't peaceful; please stop wishing for the genocide of innocent Jews with your crazy belief in the end of times! It makes your morality no different than the Nazis! You must realize that the idea of Jews in Israel being slaughtered would be a worse Holocaust!"

If they attack you, be sure that you have someone recording and have it posted online for other Indians throughout the country to see how Christians react to skeptical inquiry. Remember, if you truly care about Hinduism or any other religious faith in India, then you should be willing to take assaults peacefully. I know that doesn't sound ideal, but Gandhi and millions of other Indians, including your own family I am sure, peacefully took British beatings as a protest against colonialist occupation. If you truly want Hinduism to continue, you need to make peaceful concessions and not react in violence. I know it's hard, but please seriously consider this, these actions are the true teachings of Hinduism.

Again, be sure that you have all this filmed. Explain that your motivations for questioning the Christian missionaries were to spread freethinking and that you honestly believe Christians should confront the problems in their Bible and their strange desire for Jewish genocide which is not in the Eastern faiths and which you find morally appalling. Say that Hinduism and Judaism are the most peaceful faiths because they never warred or persecuted each other in 2400 years and that Christian history has proven the spreading of Christianity leads to persecution of Jews – just as the Portugal colonists did to Jewish Indians. Which is, in fact, the honest truth of the historical record and as such you're highlighting Hinduism's peaceful nature because Hindus and Jews never warred with each other or committed acts of religiously motivated violence upon each other. Neither Judaism nor Hinduism proselytizes.

Section 4: Transgender people, Blasphemy, and God

There have been mass killings of Transgender people in the United States. Comparatively, India has none. Question the Christian missionaries about this by asking their views on transgender people. Bring any news article of Source 6 and the article about India's superior treatment, printed out to show them what you're referring to.

1.) "Do you believe that transgender people are sinful?"

.

If they say "Yes" then show them the news article about US violence upon Transgender people.

"Then how can your religion be peaceful? We don't commit violence upon Transgenders and there have been mass killings of Transgenders by Christians in the United States. How can you allow such violence and call your religion peaceful? You seem very hateful of everyone

164

different from you. I'm glad that Indians aren't as hateful to the transgender people of our society."

If they say "No" then show them the two news articles.

"But there are mass killings of transgender people in the United States! Here's an article I found in my research! We Indians don't want to commit killings and it's proven that Christians are more likely to kill innocent transgenders. How is your faith more moral when it allows such disgusting murder sprees in a first world country? I think you are denying the clear moral failures of your religion! Why do you hate transgender people? How can you allow such hatred for others? How can Christians go on murdering whoever they want?! What is wrong with you?! Please leave, you seem to be a committed force of evil and deny your religion's moral failures which lead to deaths of innocents in the United

States and I don't want Indians here to suffer your violent

ways."

2.) "Is it okay if I call your god by his name, Yahweh?"

(pronounced "YAH – WAY")[17]

If they say "No"/Get offended/Say you should only refer

to Jesus Christ/or try to leave.

"Miss/Sir! I am only asking because you say that your

religion is more moral but how can that be when you

can't say your God's name? Blasphemy is fundamentally

against democratic belief! It is no different from a

thought crime! How can you believe in thought crimes

and blasphemy which are against democratic principles

---

[17] I deeply apologize if this offends anyone, but I sincerely believe that free thought and skeptical inquiry of Blasphemy beliefs should occur to create a better society. Blasphemy is fundamentally against the preconditions of democracy and fairness.

and have only led to mass death in Christianity's history?"

If they continue to argue with you:

"The Goa Inquisition that came from Portugal during the 1800s sliced off the body parts of peaceful Hindus in front of their families to force them to convert. They brought mass death through the belief in blasphemy and I feel that we Hindus have a right to question you to make sure that you won't hurt us like you did back then. The Goa Inquisition, the British systematic genocide, and Christian Corporations that don't provide safety regulations and allow factories to explode and kill Hindus are proof that believing in Jesus Christ doesn't lead to better moral character or moral behavior. So I feel I have a right to ask you to make sure that we're safe from any violence. Your reaction just proves you're close-minded."

If they argue those examples aren't "True Christianity":

"But all they have to do is ask Jesus for forgiveness and they can forgive themselves of any crime. How is that moral or just? In fact, it shows that being more attuned to Jesus Christ is completely meaningless. It leads to destruction and mass death, and not good moral character. Have you seen some of the forced conversions that Christian missionaries are doing? That proves that Christianity lacks good moral character!"

If they say "Yes", which would be bizarre and against their faith.

"Okay Miss/Sir, I will tell everyone that we should refer to the Christian God as Yahweh and Jesus Christ because both are equally valid names for your religion's Holy Trinity."

3.) For this next one, print out source 4, an image of Jesus Christ with signs of the Christian devil on him. Be sure to have someone with a camera to videotape the exchange. Politely introduce yourself to the Christian missionary and hand him the image.

"Do you have a problem with this image?"

If they say "Yes"

"How can Christianity be about freedom and peace when you have problems with a bunch of silly pictures? That goes against democratic freedom of expression. Why is Christianity against freedom of expression?"

If they say the image is offensive/that Christianity is not against freedom of expression/or get angry.

"Miss/Sir! Your angry reaction over a silly picture is proof that Christianity is against freedom of expression! Which is exactly my point; you shouldn't feel offended over silly pictures but clearly you don't believe in democracy, freedom of expression, and freedom of thought!"

Regarding blasphemy defense when on camera for news stations, your own videos, and filming after confrontations use the following lines or something similar to these statements:

"In a democratic country, we have a right to free speech and a right to question ideas such as blasphemy and thought crimes in religion. Christians who arrive here have threatened, assaulted, and attempted to bribe Hindus into conversions and target children in particular. These Christian fundamentalists from the US and Britain insult us by calling us devil worshippers and profess to wanting the destruction of Israel for the sake of Jesus Christ as is described within Revelations in their so-called peaceful holy book. They defend their insults through freedom of speech. We don't want anti-Semitism in our country and we are concerned for the safety of our Jewish, Transgender, and Muslim populations by these people covertly entering the country to target and harass us while they say Jewish people are evil for denying Jesus. They're doing this everywhere when there are no cameras. We know these extremist Christians aren't the majority of the West but there are enough of them to cause social and political instability with their violence. If they wish to insult our gods, then we should have the right to question the ethics of their religion because it is clear to us that they will continue their violence and coercion upon our people and especially our children. They deny their anti-Semitism on camera and are very careful when people are recording them in public but they have said some horribly anti-Semitic remarks about the Jews of Israel and India. They honestly believe Jews will be sent to hell to be judged by Satan because it is in the Christian Bible for the Coming of Jesus."

"We apologize for any offense this image is causing, but what else can we do but question Christianity when they continue to harass, assault, and threaten us and our children with beatings, rape threats, and constantly insult us by saying to our children that they're devil worshippers? If they wish to use violence, then we will question the legitimacy of their religious faith. It doesn't seem like Christians want to live in peace with anyone and the genocide of Native Americans in the US and the Holocaust of Europe is a clear indication what happens to passive innocents in Christianity's blood-soaked history."

"We are trying to be peaceful! We are trying to have rational discourse! But I'm sorry to say that none of these Christians want rational discourse and get violent when we try to talk to them peacefully. I know some instances of Hindus being violent exist, but these people are threatening our children by telling them they're going to hell for not believing in Jesus or trying to trick them into converting. They say they want to kill or convert all the Jews in India. They say they have US corporations giving them billions to wipe out all the Muslims, homosexuals, transgender people and Jews. They say that our way of life is backwards, evil, and then threaten us with violence when we try to talk it out when it's away from cameras. These people don't want peace and have shown no signs of legitimate peaceful talks. We're afraid for our minority population. They say they're going to finish what the British started and cleanse us of devil worship so that we can await a mass genocide of Jews in the holy land so the Coming of Jesus can happen."

"They say that they're funded by Evangelical billionaires and that they intend to destroy Hinduism and Islam from existence just like they did the Native Americans and Tasmanian Aboriginals. We are concerned by the horrible comments they make about transgender Indians and homosexual Indians. They say that homosexuals and transgender people are damned to hell and that they will receive God's punishment when the Jews in Israel are slaughtered by the Muslims in Islamic countries so that Jesus can come down for the rapture."

4.) "Do you truly believe that everyone who comes to Jesus Christ will be forgiven for their sins and go to heaven?"

If they say "Yes" then ask this question.

"Do you believe that even a serial killer or serial pedophile will go to heaven, if they seek Jesus's forgiveness?"

If they say "Yes" then ask 4A or 4B.

4A.) "Do you believe that any serial killer or serial rapist who kills or rapes Indian children will go to heaven if they sincerely ask for Jesus's forgiveness?"

4B.) "Do you believe that a serial killer or serial rapist

who kills or rapes your family including any children you may have will be going to heaven, if they sincerely seek Jesus Christ's forgiveness?"

If they say "Yes" to either 4B or 4A then say the following:

"Miss/Sir, that sounds like an evil God to me. What sort of moral person could see serial murderers or serial rapists going to heaven after killing innocent people? That is absolutely an evil doctrine and I believe you're wrong for preaching what are clearly evil beliefs."

If they say "No", to any of the above then say the following:

"So then, there are certain conditions in which seeking the forgiveness of your God is useless and Jesus Christ doesn't forgive everyone. Therefore, the doctrines that you preach cannot be the absolute truth and you cannot know otherwise."

If they try to argue that it is 'up to God'

"So then, certain conversions to Jesus Christ are meaningless and you cannot know if your God forgives everyone or not and it is arrogant of you to assume that you do know. So you cannot know if your conversions and your beliefs are completely meaningless or not but you pretend otherwise. You seem like a very arrogant individual to presume to know God's will and to call it humility."

Section 5: End of the World

1.) "Do you believe in the Coming of Jesus?"

   If they say "Yes", which they should otherwise they're

   not Christians.

2.) "So, you believe there will also be an apocalypse in

   which non-Christians will be killed?"

   If they say "Yes"/if they say they believe it's inevitable.

3.) "So, you believe that Jewish people who don't convert

   will all be slaughtered in a worldwide genocide that is

   worse than the Holocaust and you look forward to it

   because you believe Jesus will return?"

If they try to evade/say "No"/try to talk to someone else/or

they try to walk away.

"Miss/Sir! Are you evading my question because you secretly desire to finish what the Nazis did because you selfishly desire Jesus's return? I'm only asking because your beliefs sound anti-Semitic!"

If they get angry/if they say you're taking it out of context/evade the question/or try to walk away

4A.) "Can you not see that wanting the Jews to either convert to your faith or die is anti-Semitic? Your belief in Jesus Christ is making you anti-Semitic and blaming Jews for Jesus's death is proof of Christianity's anti-Semitism."

Or

4B.) "If Christianity is true and Jesus Christ is the Son of God, then you're saying the Jews who died in the Holocaust will be sent to hell. If they're not in hell, then there are conditions in which Jesus Christ is not needed to go to heaven and if they're in hell then your God is fundamentally evil and immoral. To argue that Jews who died in the

Holocaust are in purgatory or that it is up to God still doesn't

change this fundamental problem with the evil in your

religion!"

Chapter 6: Resources

For this section, I've chosen to add the links prior to the full description provided of the Wikipedia page or respective articles, so that people will more quickly be able to check them. I felt it was necessary to copy it all, because news articles and Wikipedia pages eventually vanish or get modified to remove pertinent and useful information. At the end of this chapter will be the PBS archaeology article and my commentary from my previous book, Faith in Doubt. If you want a fuller critique of religion and Christianity in particular (or even Islam), then I encourage you to check out that book. I don't think there's much for me to add on this section that I haven't already stated in Chapter 1, so I've decided to just keep the commentary strictly limited to the PBS article regarding the Archaeology of the Bible and lack of evidence for the story of Exodus.

NLFT Source:
https://en.wikipedia.org/wiki/National_Liberation_Front_of_Tripura

From Wikipedia, the free encyclopedia

National Liberation Front of Tripura

Participant in the Insurgency in Northeast India

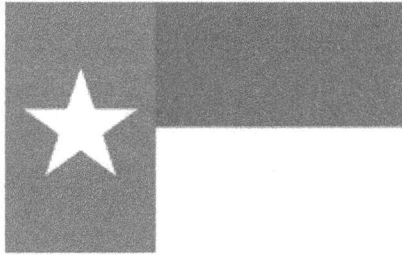

Flag of the National Liberation Front of Tripura

Active	1989 – 2019 (30 years)
Status	1996 - 2010 (14 years)
Ideology	Tripuri nationalism Separatism Christian extremism
Leaders	Biswamohan Debbarma (POW) Utpanna Tripura † Mukul Debbarma † Nayanbashi Jamatia (POW)
Headquarters	Bangladesh, Bhutan (former)

Area of operations	Tripura, India
Size	550 (Biswamohan faction)
	250 (Nayanbasi faction)
Split to	National Liberation Front of Tripura - Biswamohan, National Liberation Front of Tripura - Nayanbasi
Opponent(s)	Government of Tripura

Designated as a terrorist organisation by

Government of India,
Government of Tripura,
Interpol

The **National Liberation Front of Tripura** (abbreviated **NLFT**) is a Tripuri nationalist militant organisation based in Tripura, India. It has an estimated 550 to 850 members.

The NLFT seeks to secede from India and establish an independent Tripuri state, and is an active participant in the Insurgency in Northeast India. According to Manik Sarkar, former Chief Minister of Tripura, The NLFT manifesto says that they want to expand what they describe as the Kingdom of God and Jesus Christ in Tripura.[1]

The NLFT is currently designated as a terrorist organisation in India.[2][3]

Contents

- 1History
- 2Factions

- o   2.1Biswamohan faction
- o   2.2Nayanbasi faction
  - 3Location
  - 4Attacks
- 5Objectives/Ideologies
  - 6Peace Accord
    - 7Flag
  - 8See also
- 9References

History

The Baptist Church of Tripura was initially set up by missionaries from New Zealand in the 1940s. Despite their efforts, even until the 1980s, only a few thousand people in Tripura had converted to Christianity. In the aftermath of one of the worst ethnic riots, the NLFT was born in 1989 with the backing of the Baptist Church of Tripura.[1] Since then, the NLFT has been advancing its cause through armed rebellion. In its constitution, the organisation claims to represent the indigenous population which it claims has been marginalised by "the subjugation policy of imperialist Hindustani (India)"; its constitution makes no mention of any specific religion and claims to extend membership to "any person irrespective of caste, sex or creed".[4]

The NLFT has been described as engaging in terrorist violence motivated by their Christian beliefs.[5] The NLFT is listed as a terrorist organisation in the Prevention of Terrorism Act, 2002.[2] The state government contends that the Baptist Church of Tripura supplies arms and gives financial support to the NLFT.[3] In April 2000, according to the state government, the secretary of the Noapara Baptist Church in Tripura, Nagmanlal Halam, was arrested with explosives and confessed that for two years he had been buying explosives for the NLFT.[1] In 2000, the NLFT threatened to kill Hindus celebrating the religious festival of Durga Puja.[6] At least 20 Hindus in Tripura have been killed by the NLFT in two years for resisting forced conversion to Christianity.[7] A leader of the Jamatia tribe, Rampada Jamatia, said that armed NLFT militants were forcibly converting tribal villagers to Christianity, which he said was a serious threat to Hinduism.[7] It is believed that as many as 5,000 tribal villagers were forcibly converted from 1999 to 2001.[7] These forcible conversions to Christianity, sometimes including the use of "rape as a means of intimidation," were noted by academics outside of India in 2007.[5]

In early 2000, 16 Bengali Hindus were killed by the NLFT at Gourangatilla. On 20 May 2000, the NLFT killed 25 Bengali Hindus at the Bagber refugee camp.[8] In August 2000, a tribal Hindu spiritual leader, Shanti Kali, was shot dead by about ten NLFT guerrillas who said it wanted to convert all people in the state to Christianity.[9] In December 2000, Labh Kumar Jamatia, a religious leader of the state's second largest Hindu group, was kidnapped by the NLFT, and found dead in a forest in Dalak village in southern Tripura. According to police, rebels from the NLFT wanted Jamatia to convert to Christianity, but he refused.[10] A local Marxist tribal leader, Kishore Debbarma, was clubbed to death in Tripura's Sadar by militants from the Biswamohan faction of the NLFT in May 2005.[11]

In 2001, there were 826 reported terrorist attacks in Tripura, in which 405 people lost their lives and 481 kidnappings were made by the NLFT and related organisations such as the Christian All Tripura Tiger Force (ATTP).[12] Nagmanlal Halam, secretary of the Noapara Baptist Church in Tripura, was arrested for and confessed, under torture from police, to providing munitions and financial aid to the NLFT from 1998 until 2000.[1]

The BBC reported in 2005 that independent investigations as well as confessions from surrendered members showed that the NLFT had been making and selling pornography to finance their activities. This includes DVDs of pornographic films made by the group with tribal men and women kidnapped and forced to participate in sex acts while being filmed. The movies are dubbed into various languages and sold illegally throughout the region for a profit. Statements from former members and one report state that the NLFT has a history of sexually abusing tribal women.[13]

According to the Institute for Conflict Management, approximately 90% of the NLFT's administration are Christians.[3]

Factions

The NLFT was originally started by Dhananjoy Reang in March of 1989. Reang was removed from his position by a coup in 1993.[14] After the coup, the group was briefly led by Nayanbasi Jamatiya, and then Biswamohan Debbarma took command, but some continued to follow Nayanbasi.

Cited causes of internal conflicts[3] include the reluctance of Biswamohan Debbarma's Central Executive Committee to nominate Joshua Debbarma as the King of 'Tripura Kingdom'; misappropriation of funds by senior leaders; lavish lifestyles led by the senior leadership; and forcible conversion of tribal cadres/civilians to Christianity.

Other leaders of the original NLFT included 'Vice President' Kamini Debbarma, 'Publicity Secretary' Binoy Debbarma, 'Chief of Army' Dhanu Koloi, and 'Finance Secretary' Bishnu Prasad Jamatiya.

Biswamohan faction[edit]

The Biswamohan faction (NLFT/BM) is earlier headed by Biswamohan Debbarma. In May 2017 In a meeting at an undisclosed location, selected Subir Debbarma alias Yamorok (45), as the new 'president' of the organization renaming it as the NLFT SD. It later signed a memorandum of Settlement with Government of India to abide by The Constitution of India & join the mainstream on 10 August 2019.[15].

Upon the surrender of Mantu Koloi, second in command, he requested that Biswamohan Debbarma and Ranjit Debbarma engage in talks with the Government of India to resolve the crisis. This was sparked by the Bangladeshi government's crackdown on hostile groups. The government there were able to do this by extensively searching the Sacherri jungles where the organization had many of its hideouts.[16] However, both leaders vowed to fight on.[17]

Nayanbasi faction

The Nayanbasi faction has approximately 50 sophisticated weapons, 50 persons in collaboration with the group, and 150 cadres in active duty.[18]In January of 2004, the Nayanbasi faction group sent a message to the Additional Director of General Police (ADG) with the intention to start peace talks. These meetings ultimately were not successful. Later that year it peacefully entered into a Memorandum of Settlement with India.[19]

Location

The group has been banned from the Indian government since the Unlawful Activities Act of 1967. Therefore, the group operates from its headquarters in Khagrachari, a district in Bangladesh around 45 km from Simanapur.[20] The National Liberation Front of Tripura has the ability to utilize this 856 km of the border that is unfenced and susceptible to invasion.[21]

Attacks

The National Liberation Front of Tripura has conducted 81 attacks on various locations in South Asia and specifically in Tripura.[22] Of these 81 attacks, handguns and firearms have been the most common weapon.

The attacks that have been carried out by the NLFT have not exceeded 25 deaths. The majority of their attacks have been on citizens rather than the government although the group's main opponent is the Indian government.

Objectives/Ideologies

A common ideology within the NLFT is Tripuri Nationalism. This has two components: a Tripura state that is for only the native citizens, and the Bengalis that inhabit Tripura have no political rights or power. Among the leadership and followers of the NLFT, there are a few common objectives that come to the surface when doing analysis on this group.

1. To liberate Tripura from the union of India
2. To deport all foreigners who entered into Tripura after 1956.
3. To restore alienated tribal lands[23]

Peace Accord

Tripura Peace Accord is the tripartite accord signed-in on 10 August 2019 by the Government of India, Government of Tripura and the National Liberation Front of Tripura (NLFT) to end the insurgency.

The tripartite memorandum of understanding was signed by Satyendra Garg, Joint Secretary (Northeast) of Ministry of Home Affairs, Kumar Alok, Additional Chief Secretary (Home), Tripura and Sabir Kumar Debbarma and Kajal Debbarma of NLFT.[24]

Flag

The NLFT has its own flag which consists of three colors: green, white, and red. The green portion of the flag symbolizes sovereignty over Tripura, the land to which they lay claim. The white portion of the flag signifies the peace they desire to. The color red represents the revolution and the blood that has been shed in the name of their revolution. The final part of the flag is the star which acts as the guiding light for the Borok during this struggle.[25]

See also[edit]

- Christian terrorism
- Insurgency in Northeast India
- Separatist movements of India
- Insurgent groups in Northeast India
- Tripura Baptist Christian Union
- Indigenous Nationalist Party of Tripura
- List of terrorist organisations in India

References[edit]

1. ^ Jump up to:*a* *b* *c* *d* Bhaumik, Subir (18 April 2000). *"Church backing Tripura rebels"*. BBC News.
2. ^ Jump up to:*a* *b* *"The Prevention of Terrorism Act, 2002"*. Republic of India. South Asia Terrorism Portal. 2002.
3. ^ Jump up to:*a* *b* *c* *d* *"National Liberation Front of Tripura"*. South Asia Terrorism Portal.
4. ^ *"Constitution of The National Liberation Front Of Tripura"*. South Asia Terrorism Portal.
5. ^ Jump up to:*a* *b* Adam, Jeroen; De Cordier, Bruno; Titeca, Kristof; Vlassenroot, Koen (2007). "In the Name of the Father? Christian Terrorism in Tripura, Northern Uganda, and Ambon". Studies in Conflict and Terrorism. **30** (11): 963–83. doi:*10.1080/10576100701611288*.
6. ^ *"Separatist group bans Hindu festivities"*. BBC News. 2 October 2000.
7. ^ Jump up to:*a* *b* *c* *"Tribals unite against conversions in Tripura"*. rediff.com. 2 August 2001.
8. ^ *"19 killed in Tripura massacre rerun"*. The Telegraph. 21 May 2000.
9. ^ *"Hindu preacher killed by Tripura rebels"*. BBC News. 28 August 2000.
10. ^ *"Tripura tribal leader killed"*. BBC News. 27 December 2000.
11. ^ *"Rebels kill Tripura CPM leader"*. Telegraph India. 17 May 2005.
12. ^ *"Conversions with foreign fund"*. organiser.in. 10 April 2005. Archived from *the original* on 3 May 2005.
13. ^ Bhaumik, Subir (27 August 2005). *"India rebels 'making porn films'"*. BBC News.
14. ^ *"National Liberation Front of Tripura, India, South Asia Terrorism Porta"*. www.satp.org. Retrieved 10 April 2019.
15. ^ www.indianexpress.com*https://indianexpress.com/article/india/centre-signs-peace-pact-with-tripura-insurgent-outfit-nlft-5895406/*. Retrieved 10 August 2019.Missing or empty |title= (help)
16. ^ *"NLFT faction seeks talks"*. www.telegraphindia.com. Retrieved 23 April 2019.

17. ^ *Bhaumik, Subir (6 May 2004). "Tripura rebels surrender". BBC News.*
18. ^ *"NLFT faction willing for talks with govt | India News - Times of India". The Times of India. Retrieved 10 May 2019.*
19. ^ *"Policy for Solving Insurgency Problem in NE" (Press release). Press Information Bureau. 18 February 2009.*
20. ^ *"National Liberation Front of Tripura (NLFT) (NDFB)". www.globalsecurity.org. Retrieved 10 April 2019.*
21. ^ https://search.proquest.com/docview/1287104045
22. ^ *"GTD Search Results". www.start.umd.edu. Retrieved 11 April2019.*
23. ^ *"Constitution of National Liberation Front Of Tripura". www.satp.org. Retrieved 11 April 2019.*
24. ^ *"Peace pact signed with Tripura insurgent group". Times of India. 10 August 2019. Retrieved 10 August 2019.*
25. ^ *"Tripura (India)". www.crwflags.com. Retrieved 11 April 2019.*[18]

Source: https://www.huffpost.com/entry/ancient-mythic-origins-of_b_185455

Valerie Tarico, Contributor
Psychologist, writer, former evangelical
Ancient Sumerian Origins of the Easter Story
05/11/2009 05:12 am ET **Updated** May 25, 2011

Evangelicals across the political spectrum, from Pat Robertson to Jim Wallis, seek to shape our government and life-ways by appealing to the authority of the Christian Bible. It is virtually impossible to understand American politics without understanding the book that drives their priorities. Given that three quarters of Americans are Christians, I would argue that it is virtually impossible to move forward as a people without growing our understanding of the Book.

The Christian Bible culminates in a death and resurrection story. What is this story, and where did it come from? In this post, Valerie Tarico, author of The Dark Side, interviews Dr. Tony Nugent, scholar of world religions and mythology. Dr. Nugent is a symbologist, an expert in ancient symbols. He taught at Seattle University for fifteen years in the Department of Theology and Religious Studies and is a Presbyterian minister.

---

[18] "National Liberation Front of Tripura." Wikipedia, Wikimedia Foundation, 9 Nov. 2020, en.wikipedia.org/wiki/National_Liberation_Front_of_Tripura.

Easter is coming. Some people are saying that the crucifixion and resurrection narratives simply retell the cycle of seasons, the death and return of the Sun. Others say that these stories are literal histories. But you say the reality is more complicated than either of these. You argue that the Easter stories - the death and resurrection of Jesus have very specific mythic origins.

I view the story of Christ in the Gospels of the New Testament as a powerful and spiritually wise sacred story. While the story is told as if it happened, it is a theologically and mythically constructed history. The conclusion of the story, the account of Christ's crucifixion, resurrection and ascension to heaven, has many layers. But at its core I would say it is an historicized version of a very ancient myth from Mesopotamia, the Cradle of Civilization, the land we today call Iraq.

What does that mean?

Some stories speak to people in a deep spiritual way. These sacred stories are what are called "myths" in the field of religious studies. Despite our common usage, a myth traditionally is not just a false tale. Rather, it is a story that, at least at one point in time, had a very powerful spiritual resonance. The story of death and resurrection is one such story. In the Sumerian tradition, in which much of the Bible is rooted, the story is called, "From the Great Above to the Great Below" or "The Descent of Inanna." There is also a Babylonian version of the myth, which is called "The Descent of Ishtar," and she is known elsewhere as Astarte.

Let's hear the story!

The Sumerian goddess Inanna is the personification of the planet Venus the "Queen of Heaven" and a major deity in the Sumerian pantheon. A long, long time ago, before humans are even created, Inanna, takes a journey to the Underworld, a realm under the control of her sister Ereshkigal. Before heading out Inanna gives instructions to her assistant about rescuing her if she runs into trouble, which she does. In the underworld, she enters through seven gates, and her worldly attire is removed. "Naked and bowed low" she is judged, killed, and then hung on display.

I can't help but notice that the number seven is a sacred, just like it will be later in the Bible.

Yes, the numbers three, seven, twelve are sacred throughout ancient

Mesopotamian writings including the Hebrew Bible (seven days of creation, twelve tribes of Israel) and subsequently Christianity (three days in the tomb, twelve apostles, twelve days of Christmas). They have their roots in universal human perceptions of the movements of the heavens (e.g. twelve signs of the zodiac).

To return to the story, the result of Inanna's death is that the earth becomes sterile. Plants start drying up, and animals cease having sexual relations. Unless something is done all life on earth will end. After Inanna has been missing for three days her assistant goes to other gods for help. Finally one of them Enki, creates two creatures who carry the plant of life and water of life down to the Underworld, sprinkling them on Inanna and resurrecting her. She then prepares to return to the upper realm.

So Inanna is the prototype for Jesus in the Easter story?

Not quite. She is part of the prototype. After Inanna gets out of the underworld we are introduced to her husband Dumuzi. When mythic stories get passed from one culture to the next, sometimes one character can split into two or two characters come together. In this case, the Jesus of the resurrection story blends parts of Inanna and Dimuzi.

Ok, let's hear about Dumuzi.

The Underworld has a number of names, including "the Great Earth" and "the Great City", and it is also called the "Land of No Return." If, by extraordinary chance, someone is resurrected or escapes from there, a substitute must be provided. So when Inanna returns to the upper realm she searches for a substitute. She doesn't want to send anyone who has been missing her and mourning her down there, but she finds her husband Dumuzi on his throne and totally unconcerned about her being gone. She decides that he will be her substitute.

He protests vigorously and is helped to escape by his brother-in-law Utu, the Sun-god. But then a compromise is agreed upon, whereby Dumuzi will spend six months of every year in the Underworld, and for the other six months his devoted sister will substitute for him. Life and fertility thus return to the earth. And that's how the story ends.

Six months up and six down. Now I am reminded of Persephone.

Yes, and many other dying and rising gods that represent the cycle of the seasons and the stars. In Christianity one way the story changes is that it is detached from this agricultural cycle. The dying happens just once.

But this story of Inanna/Ishtar is the oldest, the prototype?

It is one of the earliest epic myths recorded. We know this story because it has been found inscribed on cuneiform clay tablets dug up from the sands of Iraq by archaeologists, and because linguists have deciphered the Sumerian language and provided translations in English. This was a popular myth, and so we have multiple copies of it, or of portions of it. The earliest tablets inscribed with this story date to the beginning of the 2nd millennium BC, and it is thought to have been originally formulated about 2100 BC, i.e., 4200 years ago. Politics email.

From Washington to the campaign trail, get the latest politics news. **Lay it out for us. How do you see this being a prototype for the story of Christ's death and resurrection?**

Let's start with the first part of the myth. Inanna and Jesus both travel to a big city, where they are arrested by soldiers, put on trial, convicted, sentenced to death, stripped of their clothes, tortured, hung up on a stake, and die. And then, after 3 days, they are resurrected from the dead. Now there are, to be sure, a number of significant differences between the stories. For one thing, one story is about a goddess and the other is about a divine man. But this is a specific pattern, a mythic template. When you are dealing with the question of whether these things actually happened, you have to deal with the fact that there is a mythic template here. It doesn't necessarily mean that there wasn't a real person, Jesus, who was crucified, but rather that, if there was, the story about it is structured and embellished in accordance with a pattern that was very ancient and widespread.

So what about the 2nd part of the myth?

The 2nd part of the Inanna myth really focuses on her husband Dumuzi. Dumuzi is the prototype of the non-aggressive, non-heroic male; he cries easily; he is the opposite of the warrior-god in the ancient pantheon. The summer month which corresponds to our month of July is named after him in both the Babylonian and Hebrew calendars, and during this month each year his followers, mostly women, mourn his death. From this myth we are talking about, and from a few other references, we also know that he is resurrected. But unlike Jesus, who dies and is resurrected once, he is imagined to die and be resurrected over and over, each year. There are other major differences. However, there really are a lot of similarities between the personalities and the stories of Jesus and Dumuzi. They both are tortured and die violent deaths after being betrayed by a close friend, who accepts a bribe from his enemies. They both have a father who is a god and a mother who is human. Dumuzi's father, the god Enki, also has many similarities to Yahweh, the father of Jesus.

Other than this gospel story, are there any other signs of Inanna's influence on Christianity or on Easter?

There are a few points I would mention. Inanna becomes known outside of Mesopotamia by her Babylonian name, "Ishtar". She is a personification of Venus as an evening star, and there is also a male aspect of the deity who is usually the morning star. At the end of the Book of Revelation when Christ speaks to John he says, "I am the bright morning star." In ancient Canaan Ishtar is known as Astarte, and her counterparts in the Greek and Roman pantheons are known as Aphrodite and Venus. In the 4th Century, when Christians got around to identifying the exact site in Jerusalem where the empty tomb of Jesus had been located, they selected the spot where a temple of Aphrodite (Astarte/Ishtar/Inanna) stood. So they tore it down and built the Church of the Holy Sepulchre, the holiest church in the Christian world.
Also, our holiday of Easter was traditionally called 'Pascha', and still is in many languages, named after the Jewish festival of 'Pesach' or Passover. In the Germanic and Anglo-Saxon world we have, however, come to name the holiday 'Easter'. This name is almost surely a reflex of the goddess Ishtar. In the pagan spiritual traditions of Germany and England in the medieval period Ishtar, who came to be called the goddess Easter, and who as a deity of resurrection and rebirth became strongly associated with the season of springtime and ultimately gave her name to Christianity's main holy day.

No rudeness intended, but how can you call yourself a Christian? Mark Driscoll, rising Evangelical star, told his Seattle congregation: "If the resurrection of Christ didn't literally happen, there is no reason for us to be here."

Well, many Christian theologians see the crucifixion and resurrection as a spiritual story rather than a literal one—a story about hope beyond despair, redemption and new life. But they are not the ones who get the media attention. I consider myself to be a Christian in a spiritual sense, not in a doctrinal sense. This means my Christianity is defined by values, spiritual practices, and faith rather than belief in a specific set of doctrinal agreements. Before the 4th Century, when orthodoxy was established,

Christianity was characterized by heterodoxy — many different forms of belief.

If the resurrection of Christ didn't literally happen, that shouldn't have any bearing on whether life now is worth living or how we live. From my vantage point, where values and practices are the heart of Christianity, the contradiction lies in people like our recent president who think it's ok to practice torture and yet call themselves Christians. Who would Jesus waterboard? Christ's torture and execution remind us that we are called to put an end to such practices in human affairs. From the standpoint of my Christianity, right-wing evangelical fundamentalism is really the opposite of what Christ was about. Those who subscribe to an intolerant, arrogant, inhumane form of Christianity are following a religion that is literally antichrist.[19]

Source: http://www.inanna.virtualave.net/tammuz.html

This story was inscribed on clay tablets at around 1750 BCE. The famous story of the goddess' descent into the netherworld, provides us with a testimony as to an early religion in which the goddess, woman, life and love was the center and the heart of religion.

Inanna/Ishtar's Descent

The onset of the lean season after the harvest, however brings out the fierce dark side of the goddess of death and destruction. It is celebrated by the entry of Inanna to the underworld, where she enters seven gates and her worldly attire (her signs of dominion and power) are removed (I see some relation to the dance of the seven veils here, but not the striptease kind of thing :-) and then her life is reduced to nought. Inanna decides to experience the dark side her elder sister Ereshkigal knows as Queen of the Underworld in the death rites of the Sacred Bull of Heaven, Gugalanna, thus disguising her formal purpose of discovery in the formal act of witnessing the death rites of another.

Returning from the underworld, accompanied by demons who must have a mortal in compensation, she fixes the eye of death on her absent-

---

[19] Tarico, Valerie. "Ancient Sumerian Origins of the Easter Story." HuffPost, HuffPost, 25 May 2011, www.huffpost.com/entry/ancient-mythic-origins-of_b_185455.

minded partner who is engrossed in affairs of state, and he is chased by the demons of hell, losing his possessions, his genitals and his life. Inanna afterwards laments her actions and searches for him and ensures his resurrection so that he can be brought back for six months of the year to ensure the fertility of both the womb and the soil. Seasonal male sacrifice of the "king" reverberates through the goddesses from Greece to India and over much of Africa including Cybele, Hecate and Kali. In the Sumerian view, the purpose of human life was merely to provide sustenance for the deities.

The Source:

"From the Great Above she opened her ear to the Great Below.
From the Great Above the goddess opened her ear to the Great Below.
From the Great Above Inanna opened her ear to the Great Below.

My Lady abandoned heaven and earth to descend to the underworld.
Inanna abandoned heaven and earth to descend to the underworld.
She abandoned her office of holy priestess to descend to the
underworld....

If I do not return,
Set up a lament for me by the ruins.
Beat the drum for me in the assembly places.
Circle the houses of the gods.
Tear at your eyes, at your mouth, at your thighs. ...

Go to Eridu, to the temple of Enki.
Weep before Father Enki.
Father Enki, the God of Wisdom, knows the food of life,
He knows the water of life; He knows the secrets.
Surely he will not let me die." ...

When Inanna arrived at the outer gates of the underworld, She knocked
loudly.
She cried out in a fierce voice: "Open the door, gatekeeper! Open the
door, Neti!
I alone would enter!" ...

When she entered the first gate,
the shugurra, the crown of the steppe was removed.
When she entered the second gate,

From her neck the small lapis beads were removed.
When she entered the third gate,
From her breast the double strand of beads was removed.
When she entered the fourth gate,
From her chest the breastplate called "Come, man, come!" was removed.
When she entered the fifth gate,
From her wrist the gold ring was removed.
When she entered the sixth gate,
From her hand the lapis measuring rod and line was removed.
When she entered the seventh gate,
From her body the royal robe was removed. ...

Naked and bowed low, Inanna entered the throne room.
Ereshkigal rose from her throne.
Inanna started toward the throne.
The Annuna, the judges of the underworld, surrounded her.
They passed judgment against her.
Then Ereshkigal fastened on Inanna the eye of death.
She spoke against her the word of wrath.
She uttered against her the cry of guilt.
She struck her.
Inanna was turned into a corpse,
A piece of rotting meat,
And was hung from a hook on the wall....

Then, after three days and three nights, Inanna had not returned,
Ninshubur set up a lament for her by the ruins.
She beat the drum for her in the assembly places.

Neither Enlil nor Inanna's father Nannar, the Moon God of Ur, will help her because she has craved the below, and because those who choose the underworld do not return. Ninshubur succeeds in getting Enki to secure her release:

Inanna was about to ascend from the underworld
When the Annuna, the judges of the underworld, seized her. They said:
"No one ascends from the underworld unmarked.
If Inanna wishes to return from the underworld,
She must provide someone in her place."...

As Inanna ascended from the underworld,
The galla, the demons of the underworld, clung to her side.

The galla were demons who know no food, who know no drink,
Who eat no offerings, who drink no libations,
Who accept no gifts.
They enjoy no lovemaking-
They have no sweet children to kiss.
They tear the wife from the husband's arms,
They tear the child from the father's knees,
They steal the bride from her marriage home....

The galla said: "Walk on, Inanna,
We will take Ninshubur in your place."
Inanna cried: "No! Ninshubur is my constant support...."
"Walk on to your city, Inanna, We will take Shara in your place."
Inanna cried: "No! Not Shara! He is my son who sings hymns to me. ...
"Walk on to your city, Inanna, We will take Lulal in your place."
"Not Lulal! He is my son. He is a leader among men. ...
"Walk on to your city, Inanna.
We will go with you to the big apple tree in Uruk."
In Uruk, by the big apple tree,

Dumuzi, the husband of Inanna, was dressed in his shining me-garments.
He sat on his magnificent throne; (he did not move).
The galla seized him by his thighs.
They poured milk out of his seven churns.
They broke the reed pipe which the shepherd was playing.

Inanna fastened on Dumuzi the eye of death.
She spoke against him the word of wrath.
She uttered against him the cry of guilt:
"Take bim! Take Dumuzi away!"

The galla, who know no food, who know no drink,
Who eat no offerings, who drink no libations,
Who accept no gifts, seized Dumuzi.
They made him stand up; they made him sit down.
They beat the husband of Inanna.
They gashed him with axes."

The Story in Short:

Ishtar thinks to go into the Place of Darkness in search of her beloved
spouse Tammuz. Arrayed in her magnificent power and splendor she

196

enters the cavern that leads to that realm. The place is surrounded by seven walls and has seven gates and at her demand for entry, the watchman, Nedu, begs leave to consult with his mistress, Irkalla, sister of Ishtar. The mistress of the Place of Darkness bids Nedu to admit Ishtar in accordance with the ancient rites.

1. At the first gate he removes her splendid crown.
2. At the second gate he removes her necklace with the eight-rayed star.
3. At the third gate he removes her bracelets of gold and lapis lazuli.
4. At the fourth gate he removes her shoes.
5. At the fifth gate he removes her veil.
6. At the sixth gate he removes her outer robe.
7. At the seventh gate he removes her garment.

"And naked, with her splendor, and her power, and her beauty all gone from her, the Lady of the Gods came before Irkalla. And Irkalla, the goddess of the World Below, had the head of a lioness and the body of a woman; in her hands she grasped a serpent."

Irkala curses Ishtar and summons the plague demon to afflict her. And Ishtar becomes as one dead -- "Ishtar saw the light no more; feathers came upon her; she ate dust and fed upon mud...." Meanwhile Shamash, Lord of the Sun, notices the effect of Ishtar's absence on the world and concludes that this generation of creatures will die and that the creation will end. He sends Ea to conjure the Water of Life from Irkalla, and revive Ishtar. This Ea does through an intermediary.[20]

Source: https://www.gotquestions.org/how-many-angels-are-there.html

How many angels are there?

Question: "How many angels are there?"

Answer: Only three angels are identified by name in the Bible: Gabriel (Daniel 8:16), Michael the archangel (Daniel 10:13), and Lucifer the fallen angel (Isaiah 14:12). Yet angelic beings are

---

[20] Ishtar's Descent into the Underworld (Page 1), www.inanna.virtualave.net/tammuz.html.

197

mentioned at least 273 times in 34 books of the Bible. While we don't know exactly how many angels there are, we do know from Scripture that an exceedingly large number of angels exist.

The book of Hebrews describes a multitude of angels in heaven that are too great to count: "You have come to Mount Zion, to the city of the living God, the heavenly Jerusalem, and to countless thousands of angels in a joyful gathering" (Hebrews 12:22, NLT). Other Bible translations use terms like "innumerable" (ESV), "myriads" (CSB), and "thousands upon thousands" (NIV) to quantify this enormous throng of angels. The impressive picture expands in the book of Revelation: "Then I looked and heard the voice of many angels, numbering thousands upon thousands, and ten thousand times ten thousand. They encircled the throne and the living creatures and the elders" (Revelation 5:11). Other Bible versions use "myriads of myriads" (ESV) and even "millions" (NLT) here to express how many angels there are in heaven.

While the Bible leaves the precise number of angels unspecified, some believe there could be as many angels in existence as the total number of humans in all of history. This theory is based on Matthew 18:10: "Beware that you don't look down on any of these little ones. For I tell you that in heaven their angels are always in the presence of my heavenly Father" (NLT). The passage seems to suggest that individual people, or at least children, have guardian angels to protect them. It's possible, though, that Jesus was speaking here only in general terms regarding the function of angels as protectors of children. In any case, Scripture is clear that angels do guard and protect human beings (Psalm 34:7; 91:11–12; Matthew 18:10; Acts 12:9–15).

The Bible describes different classifications of angels. Some angels—the cherubim and seraphim—are described as winged creatures. Cherubim primarily attend the throne of God as guards, while it seems the seraphim attend His throne by offering worship and praise. (Ezekiel 1:4–28; 10:1–22; Isaiah 6:2–6). The Bible speaks of angels of light (2 Corinthians 11:14) and fallen angels (2 Peter 2:4; Jude 1:6).

Angels perform different tasks in the Bible. Some angels are God's messengers (Daniel 4:13). Other angels are servants of God (Psalm 103:20; Hebrews 1:7; Psalm 104:4). "Watcher angels" are mentioned in the book of Daniel (Daniel 4:13, 17, 23). Angels are often described as military "hosts" of the celestial armies (Jeremiah 5:14; 38:17; 44:7; Hosea 12:5). Other times angels are called "sons of the mighty" (Psalm 89:6) or "sons of God" (Job 2:1).

A few passages of Scripture describe angels as stars (Revelation 9:1; 12:4; Job 38:7–8; Daniel 8:10; Judges 5:20). The idea of stars may give us our best clue as to how many angels there are. If angels are like the stars in heaven, they are too many to count. Moses says in Deuteronomy 33:2 that the Lord came to speak to him from Sinai with "myriads of holy ones," or angels. How many are myriads? The primary definition of *myriad* as an adjective is "innumerable," or "countless." Psalm 68:17 says the angels of God number "tens of thousands, thousands and thousands" (CSB). Clearly, the writer has trouble even coming close to estimating the number of angels in existence.[21]

From Part II of my book, Faith in Doubt:

For a more thorough explanation, PBS.org provided an interview about "*The Archaeology of the Hebrew Bible*" on their NOVA program with the lead researcher of archaeological excavations. Please keep in mind, the archaeological research was done for over thirty years in order to prove the Bible's history was real:

---

[21] "How Many Angels Are There?" GotQuestions.org, 13 May 2019, www.gotquestions.org/how-many-angels-are-there.html.

Archeology of the Hebrew Bible

William Dever, Professor Emeritus at the University of Arizona, has investigated the archeology of the ancient Near East for more than 30 years and authored almost as many books on the subject. In the following interview, Dever describes some of the most significant archeological finds related to the Hebrew Bible, including his own hot-button discovery that the Israelites' God was linked to a female goddess called Asherah.

PROVING THE BIBLE

NOVA: Have biblical archeologists traditionally tried to find evidence that events in the Bible really happened?

William Dever: From the beginnings of what we call biblical archeology, perhaps 150 years ago, scholars, mostly western scholars, have attempted to use archeological data to prove the Bible. And for a long time it was thought to work. [William Foxwell] Albright, the great father of our discipline, often spoke of the "archeological revolution." Well, the revolution has come but not in the way that Albright thought. The truth of the matter today is that archeology raises more questions about the historicity of the Hebrew Bible and even the New Testament than it provides answers, and that's very disturbing to some people.

But perhaps we were asking the wrong questions. I have always thought that if we resurrected someone from the past, one of the biblical writers, they would be amused, because for them it would have made no difference. I think they would have said, faith is faith is faith—take your proofs and go with them.

The fact is that archeology can never prove any of the theological suppositions of the Bible. Archeologists can often tell you what happened and when and where and how and even why. No archeologists can tell anyone what it means, and most of us don't try.

Yet many people want to know whether the events of the Bible are real, historic events.

We want to make the Bible history. Many people think it has to be history or nothing. But there is no word for history in the Hebrew Bible. In other words, what did the biblical writers think they were doing? Writing objective history? No. That's a modern discipline. They were telling stories. They wanted you to know what these purported events mean.

The Bible is didactic literature; it wants to teach, not just to describe. We try to make the Bible something it is not, and that's doing an injustice to the biblical writers. They were good historians, and they could tell it the way it was when they wanted to, but their objective was always something far beyond that.

I like to point out to my undergraduate students that the Bible is not history; it's *his* story—Yahweh's story, God's story. [Yahweh is an ancient Israelite name for God.]

Even if archeology can't prove events of the Bible, can it enhance our understanding of the Bible?

Archeology is almost the only way that we have for reconstructing a real-life context for the world out of which the Bible came, and that does bring understanding. When you think of how little we knew about the biblical world even 100 years ago and what we know today, it's astonishing.

THE FAITH OF ABRAHAM

According to the Bible, the first person to form a covenant with God is Abraham. He is the great patriarch. Is there archeological evidence for Abraham?

One of the first efforts of biblical archeology in the last century was to prove the historicity of the patriarchs, to locate them in a particular period in the archeological history. Today I think most archeologists would argue that there is no direct archeological proof that Abraham, for instance, ever lived. We do know a lot about pastoral nomads, we know about the Amorites' migrations from Mesopotamia to Canaan, and it's possible to see in that an Abraham-like figure somewhere around 1800 B.C.E. But there's no direct connection.

Are we to become unbelievers if we can't prove that Abraham ever lived? What is the story about? It's a story about freedom and faith and risk. Does it matter exactly how Abraham and his clan left, and when they arrived in Canaan, or where they settled? What really matters is that Abraham is seen later by Jews and Christians as the father of the faithful.

Abraham moves out on faith to a land he has never seen. You have to think of how perilous the journey would have been had it really taken place. We are talking about a journey of several hundred miles around the fringes of the desert. So it's an astonishing story. Is it true? It is profoundly true, but it's not the kind of truth that archeology can directly illuminate.

Why is it difficult for archeologists to find support for the accounts of the patriarchs?

It disturbs some people that, for the very early periods such as the so-called patriarchal period, we archeologists haven't much to say. The later we come in time, the firmer the ground we stand on—we have better sources. We have more written sources. We have more contemporary eyewitness sources.

For the earlier periods, we don't have any texts. Abraham might have lived around 1800 B.C.E. This is the dawn of written history or prehistory, when the archeological evidence can't easily be correlated with any external evidence, textual evidence—even if we did have it.

EVIDENCE OF THE EARLY ISRAELITES

The Bible chronology puts Moses much later in time, around 1450 B.C.E. Is there archeological evidence for Moses and the mass exodus of hundreds of thousands of Israelites described in the Bible?

We have no direct archeological evidence. "Moses" is an Egyptian name. Some of the other names in the narratives are Egyptian, and there are genuine Egyptian elements. But no one has found a text or an artifact in Egypt itself or even in the Sinai that has any direct connection. That doesn't mean it didn't happen. But I think it does mean what happened was rather more modest. And the biblical writers have enlarged the story.

[For more on Moses and the Exodus, see Carol Meyer's interview.]

Is there mention of the Israelites anywhere in ancient Egyptian records?

No Egyptian text mentions the Israelites except the famous inscription of Merneptah dated to about 1206 B.C.E. But those Israelites were in Canaan; they are not in Egypt, and nothing is said about them escaping from Egypt.

Tell us more about the Merneptah inscription. Why is it so famous?
It's the earliest reference we have to the Israelites. The victory stele of Pharaoh Merneptah, the son of Ramesses II, mentions a list of peoples and city-states in Canaan, and among them are the Israelites. And it's interesting that the other entities, the other ethnic groups, are described as nascent states, but the Israelites are described as "a people." They have not yet reached a level of state organization.

So the Egyptians, a little before 1200 B.C.E., know of a group of people somewhere in the central highlands—a loosely affiliated tribal confederation, if you will—called "Israelites." These are our Israelites. So this is a priceless inscription.

Does archeology back up the information in the Merneptah inscription? Is there evidence of the Israelites in the central highlands of Canaan at this time?

We know today, from archeological investigation, that there were more than 300 early villages of the 13th and 12th century in the area. I call these "proto-Israelite" villages.

Forty years ago it would have been impossible to identify the earliest Israelites archeologically. We just didn't have the evidence. And then, in a series of regional surveys, Israeli archeologists in the 1970s began to find small hilltop villages in the central hill country north and south of Jerusalem and in lower Galilee. Now we have almost 300 of them.

THE ORIGINS OF ISRAEL

What have archeologists learned from these settlements about the early Israelites? Are there signs that the Israelites came in conquest, taking over the land from Canaanites?

The settlements were founded not on the ruins of destroyed Canaanite towns but rather on bedrock or on virgin soil. There was no evidence of armed conflict in most of these sites. Archeologists also have discovered that most of the large Canaanite towns that were supposedly destroyed by invading Israelites were either not destroyed at all or destroyed by "Sea People"—Philistines, or others.

So gradually the old conquest model [based on the accounts of Joshua's conquests in the Bible] began to lose favor amongst scholars. Many scholars now think that most of the early Israelites were originally Canaanites, displaced Canaanites, displaced from the lowlands, from the river valleys, displaced geographically and then displaced ideologically.

So what we are dealing with is a movement of peoples but not an invasion of an armed corps from the outside. A social and economic revolution, if you will, rather than a military revolution. And it begins a slow process in which the Israelites distinguish themselves from their Canaanite ancestors, particularly in religion—with a new deity, new religious laws and customs, new ethnic markers, as we would call them today.

If the Bible's story of Joshua's conquest isn't entirely historic, what is its meaning?

Why was it told? Well, it was told because there were probably armed conflicts here and there, and these become a part of the story glorifying the career of Joshua, commander in chief of the Israelite forces. I suspect that there is a historical kernel, and there are a few sites that may well have been destroyed by these Israelites, such as Hazor in Galilee, or perhaps a site or two in the south.

Were the people who became Israelites in some sense not "the chosen people" but rather "the choosing people"—choosing to be free of their Canaanite past?

Some liberation theologians and some archeologists have argued that early Israel was a kind of revolutionary social movement. These were people rebelling against their corrupt Canaanite overlords. In my recent book on early Israel I characterize the Israelite movement as an agrarian social reform. These are pioneers in the hill country who are fleeing the urban centers, the old Canaanite cities, which are in a process of collapse. And in particular they are throwing off the yoke of their Canaanite and Egyptian overlords. They are declaring independence.

Now, why these people were willing to take such a risk, colonizing the hill country frontier, is very difficult to know. I think there were social and economic compulsions, but I would be the first to say I think it was probably also a new religious vision.

Was this an egalitarian movement?

Some have argued that early Israel was an egalitarian society, that there was no social stratification. I'm not sure any society was ever really egalitarian, but there is a sort of egalitarianism in the Hebrew Bible: "Every man under his own fig tree, equal in the eyes of Yahweh." It's interesting that in these hundreds of 12th-century settlements there are no temples, no palaces, no elite residences, no monumental architecture of any kind. These are farming villages in which every household is independent. I think there is a kind of primitive democracy in early Israel, which is enshrined in the vision of the good life in the Hebrew Bible.

And these settlements grow, right?

Yes. These settlements are very different from the urban centers of the earlier 13th century. Something new is in the air, and I think this explains why other people join this movement. These villages will develop into the towns and the cities of the later state of Israel.

A UNITED MONARCHY

When did Israel become a state?

According to the biblical scheme of events, there was a United Monarchy for about a hundred years in the reigns of Saul, David, and Solomon. Then a civil war brought about the division of the country into Israel, the northern kingdom, and Judah, the southern kingdom. Now, some skeptics today have argued that there was no such thing as a United Monarchy. In short, there was no David.

However, in 1993 an inscription was found at Tel Dan. It mentions a dynasty of David. And on the Mesha stone found in the last century in Moab there is also a probable reference to David. So there is textual evidence outside the Bible for these kings of the United Monarchy, at least David.

Most of us mainstream archeologists also have now dated a series of monumental royal constructions to the 10th century—the famous gates at Hazor and Megiddo and Gezer. And we have in the Bible, in First Kings

9:15-17, the famous description of Solomon's construction of gates of Jerusalem, Hazor, Megiddo, and Gezer. So I would argue for a 10th-century United Monarchy.

The Bible describes it as a glorious kingdom stretching from Egypt to Mesopotamia. Does archeology back up these descriptions?

The stories of Solomon are larger than life. According to the stories, Solomon imported 100,000 workers from what is now Lebanon. Well, the whole population of Israel probably wasn't 100,000 in the 10th century. Everything Solomon touched turned to gold. In the minds of the biblical writers, of course, David and Solomon are ideal kings chosen by Yahweh. So they glorify them.

Now, archeology can't either prove or disprove the stories. But I think most archeologists today would argue that the United Monarchy was not much more than a kind of hill-country chiefdom. It was very small-scale.

Does archeology in Jerusalem itself reveal anything about the Kingdom of David and Solomon?

We haven't had much of an opportunity to excavate in Jerusalem. It's a living city, not an archeological site. But we have a growing collection of evidence—monumental buildings that most of us would date to the 10th century, including the new so-called Palace of David. Having seen it with the excavator, it is certainly monumental. Whether it's a palace or an administrative center or a combination of both or a kind of citadel remains to be seen.

[Hear the excavator herself, Eilat Mazar, describe the Palace of David.]

THE ISRAELITES' MANY GODS

The Bible would have us think that all Israelites embraced monotheism relatively early, from Moses's time on. Is that contrary to what archeology has found?
The portrait of Israelite religion in the Hebrew Bible is the ideal, the ideal in the minds of those few who wrote the Bible—the elites, the Yahwists, the monotheists. But it's not the ideal for most people. And archeology deals with the ordinary, forgotten folk of ancient Israel who have no voice in the Bible. There is a wonderful phrase in Daniel Chapter 12:

"For all those who sleep in the dust." Archeology brings them to light and allows them to speak. And most of them were not orthodox believers.

However, we should have guessed already that polytheism was the norm and not monotheism from the biblical denunciations of it. It was real and a threat as far as those who wrote the Bible were concerned. And today archeology has illuminated what we could call "folk religion" in an astonishing manner.

One of the astonishing things is your discovery of Yahweh's connection to Asherah. Tell us about that.

In 1968, I discovered an inscription in a cemetery west of Hebron, in the hill country, at the site of Khirbet el-Qí´m, a Hebrew inscription of the 8th century B.C.E. It gives the name of the deceased, and it says "blessed may he be by Yahweh"—that's good biblical Hebrew—but it says "by Yahweh and his Asherah."

Asherah is the name of the old Canaanite Mother Goddess, the consort of El, the principal deity of the Canaanite pantheon. So why is a Hebrew inscription mentioning Yahweh in connection with the Canaanite Mother Goddess? Well, in popular religion they were a pair.

The Israelite prophets and reformers denounce the Mother Goddess and all the other gods and goddesses of Canaan. But I think Asherah was widely venerated in ancient Israel. If you look at Second Kings 23, which describes the reforms of King Josiah in the late 7th century, he talks about purging the Temple of all the cult paraphernalia of Asherah. So the so-called folk religion even penetrated the Temple in Jerusalem.

Is there other evidence linking Asherah to Yahweh?

In the 1970s, Israeli archeologists digging in Kuntillet Ajrud in the Sinai found a little desert fort of the same period, and lo and behold, we have "Yahweh and Asherah" all over the place in the Hebrew inscriptions.

Are there any images of Asherah?

For a hundred years now we have known of little terracotta female figurines. They show a nude female; the sexual organs are not represented but the breasts are. They are found in tombs, they are found in households, they are found everywhere. There are thousands of them. They date all the way from the 10th century to the early 6th century.

They have long been connected with one goddess or another, but many scholars are still hesitant to come to a conclusion. I think they are representations of Asherah, so I call them Asherah figurines.

There aren't such representations of Yahweh, are there?

No. Now, why is it that you could model the female deity but not the male deity? Well, I think the First and Second Commandments by now were taken pretty seriously. You just don't portray Yahweh, the male deity, but the Mother Goddess is okay. But his consort is probably a lesser deity.

We found molds for making Asherah figurines, mass-producing them, in village shrines. So probably almost everybody had one of these figurines, and they surely have something to do with fertility. They were no doubt used to pray for conceiving a child and bearing the child safely and nursing it. It's interesting to me that the Israelite and Judean ones are rather more modest than the Canaanite ones, which are right in your face. The Israelite and Judean ones mostly show a nursing mother.

This has been something of a lightning rod, has it not?
This is awkward for some people, the notion that Israelite religion was not exclusively monotheistic. But we know now that it wasn't. Monotheism was a late development. Not until the Babylonian Exile and beyond does Israelite and Judean religion—Judaism—become monotheistic.

THE IMPROBABLE RISE OF JUDAISM

Does archeology have evidence of the destruction of Jerusalem by the Babylonians?
When it comes to destructions that might be illuminated by archeology, none would be more important than the destruction of Jerusalem and the Temple in 586 B.C.E. by the Babylonians. Unfortunately, we don't have a lot of direct archeological evidence because we have never been able to excavate large areas in Jerusalem. The late Israeli archeologist Yigal Shiloh found a huge accumulation of debris on the east side of the Temple Mount, cascaded down the hill. So there is some evidence, not

yet well-published. Of course, the Temple Mount has never been excavated and never will be.

That doesn't mean that that the destruction didn't take place and that it wasn't a watershed event. One would have thought at that time that it was the end of the people of Israel—with elites carried away into captivity and ordinary people impoverished. It would have seemed to have been the end, but it was rather the beginning. Because it was in exile, precisely, that those who wrote the Bible looked back, collected the archives they had, rethought it all, reformulated it, and out of that intellectual reconstruction comes early Judaism.

It seems astonishing that after this defeat the Israelites could stay faithful to their god.

In every age of disbelief, one is inclined to think that God is dead. And surely those who survived the fall of Jerusalem must have thought so. After all, how could God allow his Temple, his house—the visible sign of his presence amongst his people—to be destroyed? What did we do wrong? It's out of this that comes the reflection that polytheism was our downfall. There is, after all, only one God. And this radical belief in a single God who governs history becomes the heart of Judaism[22]

Unfortunately for people of the Abrahamic faiths, the

evidence shows that this God of the Covenant never existed and the

events of being freed from slavery simply never happened. There

was no covenant with any God and that is the central foundation of

the Jewish faith. There was never any need to be freed from slavery,

because the Israelites were never enslaved by the Egyptians. If

Passover isn't based upon a real historical event, then absolutely

---

[22] "Archeology of the Hebrew Bible." *PBS*, Public Broadcasting Service, 18 Nov. 2008, www.pbs.org/wgbh/nova/ancient/archeology-hebrew-bible.html.

none of it matters. The persecution, the freedom from slavery, or the supposed evils of the Pharaohs have no historical credibility. There's no point in celebrating the blessings of a God for miracles that never happened and were never necessary to begin with. *The Abrahamic God never displayed any miracles of freedom nor is the Mosiac Law bound by any covenant with a deity at all.* This "revealed wisdom" is a complete fairytale made for ancient political ends to kill and conquer for territory and that history of violence is shown everyday in our contemporary time with the Israel-Palestine conflict. A pointless theological conflict grounded in imaginary covenants and promises from the same deity that both claim to be the true followers of, but which neither can claim to be chosen people of since the Prophet Moses never existed and the events of the Exodus have been proven false on the basis of physical evidence. *In effect, the Israeli-Palestine conflict is people murdering each other over a fairytale in every sense of the word.* The lack of evidence for the Exodus disproves the entirety of the Abrahamic religious traditions. *It's simply indefensible and illogical to continue believing, dying, and killing for a tradition that is a falsehood. There's no meaning or greater purpose in it.* To continue this route of believing in the Bible's contents despite the overwhelming archeological findings is the very act of willful ignorance. Blind faith and willful ignorance are shown to be the same exact concept when faced with the overwhelming fact that there's no credible evidence for the Exodus story.

&

Sources for the **Chapter 5 Questions**:

If you have a computer, then please do a search of these links to read or view all materials to better understand where Evangelical Christians are coming from, their objectives, and the abuses of modern Christians that remain hidden from the public.

ALL LINKS ARE CAN ONLY BE READ IN ENGLISH

One of the places where Christian missionaries are gaining their finances from:

http://www.forbes.com/sites/briansolomon/2012/09/18/david-green-the-biblical-billionaire-backing-the-evangelical-movement/

Each of the sources will be below the brief summary:

Source 1: The mass rapes of Native Americans ongoing in the United States even after their culture was destroyed and they were forced to convert to Christianity under false promises of a better life. 80% of the perpetrators of these massive rapes that the Western media hides come from US citizens and the perpetrators are overwhelmingly US citizens that have no affiliation with Native Americans. Statistically speaking, it's highly likely that all or most of the perpetrators of these rapes are Christians. In particular, I recommend reading Chapter 4 to its totality.

http://www.amnestyusa.org/pdfs/MazeOfInjustice.pdf

Source 2: There are mass killings, rapes, and assaults on Christian women by their Christian husbands in South Carolina. They use the Bible as the primary guide for living. Many Christian missionaries who come to India are from South Carolina and might have a criminal record of abusing women. Christian men from this specific part of the US feel they have a right to assault, rape, and murder their wives because of the Bible's teachings of men being in charge of the household as if they're God.

http://www.postandcourier.com/tilldeath/title.html

http://www.postandcourier.com/tilldeath/partone.html

Source 3: Jehovah's Witnesses have been found to have hidden massive child rape cases throughout the United States and the world. They continue to deny the mounting evidence and allegations of their pastors forcibly raping their own children and using their religious organizations to hide the events.

https://www.revealnews.org/article/jehovahs-witnesses-use-1st-amendment-to-hide-child-sex-abuse-claims/

http://www.mirror.co.uk/news/uk-news/jehovahs-witnesses-sex-abuse-scandal-4422943

http://www.huffingtonpost.com/2015/02/18/jehovahs-witness-child-sex-abuse_n_6705852.html

Source 4: This is considered a blasphemous image to Christians and is clearly against the idea of freedom of thought, freedom of expression, and democratic principles.

http://images3.wikia.nocookie.net/__cb20060425134008/uncycloped ia/images/0/07/Evil_jesus.jpg

Source 5:

A documentary on the objective of Evangelical Christians and their beliefs:

https://www.youtube.com/watch?v=nNvtA_q0e20

I suggest purchasing copies of this film to show to fellow Dharmic worshippers or any Muslim friends you may have, in case it is removed. American Evangelicals explain, in detail, that they wish for a massive Holocaust worse than Hitler's genocide of Jews so that Jesus Christ can come fly them to a new world after all non-Christians face doom in some apocalypse. That is the primary motivator of Christian conversions.

Source 6:

News articles of transgender killings in the US.

http://time.com/3999348/transgender-murders-2015/

http://www.washingtonpost.com/news/morning-mix/wp/2015/08/14/transgender-killings-on-the-rise-this-is-just-so-crazy/

http://www.nytimes.com/2015/08/21/us/explosion-of-transgender-murders-contrast-with-growing-acceptance.html

News article proving Indian tolerance of the Transgender community in India, which is superior to the US:

https://www.washingtonpost.com/posteverything/wp/2015/01/29/india-has-outlawed-homosexuality-but-its-better-to-be-transgender-there-than-in-the-u-s/

&

A short list of the Catholic Church's child rape scandals across the world with sources you can look up at your own time:

UK Birmingham Archdiocese permissive attitude towards pedophile priests: https://www.independent.co.uk/news/uk/home-news/catholic-church-child-sex-abuse-birmingham-archdiocese-paedophile-priests-a8967426.html

2 of UK's leading Catholic Schools have culture of acceptance of sexual abuse of children: https://www.theguardian.com/society/2018/aug/09/report-damns-culture-of-acceptance-of-sexual-abuse-at-two-catholic-schools

German Catholic Churches cover-up of Child Rape Crimes: https://apnews.com/8e627156352a4d9fb2ad95c4353882e3

7 Percent of Australia's Catholic Priests accused of sexually abusing

children: https://www.pbs.org/newshour/world/7-percent-of-

australias-catholic-priests-accused-of-sexually-abusing-children

Chilean child rape scandal by Catholic Church:
https://www.reuters.com/article/us-chile-abuse/chileans-lose-faith-
as-vatican-scrambles-to-contain-sex-abuse-scandal-
idUSKCN1G72IJ

https://www.usnews.com/news/best-countries/articles/2018-06-
05/abuse-scandals-erode-authority-of-catholic-church-in-chile

Dutch Catholic Church's widespread cover-up of child rape and

abuse for over 65 years:

https://www.theguardian.com/world/2018/sep/16/dutch-catholic-

church-accused-of-widespread-cover--up

https://www.cnn.com/2011/12/16/world/europe/netherlands-church-

sex-abuse/index.html

Endemic rape and abuse of children in Catholic Church care within

Ireland: https://www.theguardian.com/world/2009/may/20/irish-

catholic-schools-child-abuse-claims

Rape Crimes in Catholic Orphanages in Ireland:

https://www.theguardian.com/world/2009/may/20/irish-catholic-schools-child-abuse-claims

Child Rape of Dead and Mute Boys in Catholic Church run Deaf and Mute School: https://www.thedailybeast.com/the-sex-abuse-of-deaf-orphans-in-pope-francis-backyard?ref=wrap

Catholic Bishop raped Nun 13 times in India and then the Catholic Church ordered the Nun who initially spoke out to be silent: https://www.theglobeandmail.com/world/article-indian-bishop-charged-with-repeatedly-raping-nun-2/

https://www.theguardian.com/world/2018/sep/10/indian-catholic-nuns-protest-bishop-franco-mullackal-accused-of-rape

https://www.independent.co.uk/news/world/asia/india-nun-rape-bishop-sexual-abuse-trial-franco-mulakka-kerala-catholic-church-a8772596.html

Physical and Sexual abuse of Native American children at Catholic Residential schools in Canada:

https://www.theguardian.com/world/2015/jun/06/canada-dark-of-history-residential-schools

US Catholic Church cases of the Rape and Abuse of children: 200 Deaf Boys raped in Wisconsin by Milwaukee Archdiocese:

https://www.telegraph.co.uk/news/worldnews/europe/vaticancityandholysee/7521227/Pope-accused-of-covering-up-abuse-of-200-boys.html

Montana's Native American Reservations were "dumping grounds" for pedophile priests:

https://www.greatfallstribune.com/story/news/2017/08/16/montanas-reservations-were-dumping-grounds-predatory-priests-suit-alleges/504576001/

Texas child abuse by pedophile Catholic Priests:

https://www.nbcnews.com/news/us-news/hundreds-accused-abusers-named-catholic-leaders-texas-n965716

West Virginia Lawsuit over pedophile Catholic Priests:

https://www.usnews.com/news/national-news/articles/2019-03-19/west-virginia-sues-catholic-church-for-covering-up-sex-abuse

Pennsylvania Grand Jury Report on Pedophile Priests:

https://newrepublic.com/minutes/150676/it-happened-everywhere-unimaginable-scale-sexual-abuse-pennsylvanias-catholic-church

Rape and abuse of children in Minnesota by Catholic Nuns:

https://www.foxnews.com/us/the-dark-silent-history-of-nuns-sexually-abusing-minors-set-to-become-the-next-church-scandal

Sexual violence against children in Catholic schools in New Jersey:

https://www.huffpost.com/entry/catholic-boys-school-acknowledges-sexual-abuse_n_5b59d8dce4b0fd5c73ccaec0

Vermont Child Abuse at St. Joseph's Catholic Orphanage:

https://www.buzzfeednews.com/article/christinekenneally/orphanage-death-catholic-abuse-nuns-st-josephs

What happened in Native American Boarding Schools:

https://www.npr.org/templates/story/story.php?storyId=16516865

Actions by the Catholic Church in Chronological Order in more

recent years:

2017: They Quietly Trimmed Sanctions on Child Rapists:

https://apnews.com/64e1fc2312764a24bf1b2d6ec3bf4caf

August 2018:

Catholic Church paid out nearly $4 billion of its donated money over

allegations of child rape and other abuses by pedophile priests:

https://www.newsweek.com/over-3-billion-paid-lawsuits-catholic-

church-over-sex-abuse-claims-1090753

Australia Catholic Church Rejected Calls for Priests to report Child

Rapists to go to the police due to the Seal of Confession as part of

their faith in Jesus Christ:

https://www.cnn.com/2018/08/30/australia/australia-catholic-church-

response-intl/index.html

November 2018: Vatican used their authority to stop US bishops

from voting on reforms for Catholic Churches in the US:

https://www.cnn.com/2018/11/12/us/conference-of-catholic-bishops-vatican/index.html

December 2018, Pope Francis makes a speech about how Clerics should hand themselves in, but no steps for reform are made: https://www.cnn.com/2018/12/21/europe/pope-francis-sex-abuse-church-intl/index.html

February 2019, German Cardinal Reinhard Marx admits that documents pertaining to child rape and other forms of child abuse by Catholic clergy were destroyed, tampered with, or never made: https://www.cnn.com/2019/02/23/europe/cardinal-documents-destroyed/index.html

June 2019: Catholic Church spent $10 million on lobbyists to prevent victims of child rape and other sexual abuses to sue the Catholic Church by reforming the Statue of Limitations in the US: https://www.nbcnews.com/news/us-news/catholic-church-spent-10-million-lobbyists-fight-stymie-priest-sex-n1013776

Sept 2019: Research indicates that Catholic Church was raping kids prior to the Vatican II summit. It contradicts the claim that sexual revolution of the West in the 1960s was the cause of pedophilia in the Catholic Church. This is due to the child rape in Catholic Churches being a global phenomenon with reports of child rape existing prior to those events:

https://berkleycenter.georgetown.edu/responses/clerical-sexual-abuse-religious-institutions-must-have-a-pentecost-moment-and-they-must-have-it-now

October 2019: Report finds that approximately 1700 Catholic clergy members credibly accused of child rape remain near children in unsupervised roles throughout the US. Roles listed in the article as examples are Math teachers, nurses, sexual assault counselors, and non-profit volunteers:

https://www.nbcnews.com/news/religion/nearly-1-700-priests-clergy-accused-sex-abuse-are-unsupervised-n1062396

July 2020: Catholic Church lobbied for US taxpayer funds and got between $1.4 billion and 3.5 billion due to COVID-19 pandemic relief. This was reportedly alongside other religious institutions:

https://apnews.com/article/dab8261c68c93f24c0bfc1876518b3f6

Nov 2020: Catholic Church in England and Wales, UK found to have swept credible accusations of child rape under the rug to protect pedophile Catholic priests:

https://www.theguardian.com/world/2020/nov/10/child-sexual-abuse-in-catholic-church-swept-under-the-carpet-inquiry-finds

Feb 2021: Scandal reveals German Nuns sold Orphan children to sexual predators:

https://www.thedailybeast.com/german-nuns-sold-orphaned-children-to-sexual-predators-says-report

March 2021, Catholic Church lobbied against suicide prevention of LGBT:

&

This final portion of the chapter is set towards showing the frankly pathetic desperation by even accredited professionals to find "meaning" and "value" in the cultural hoax that is the Exodus story. I've decided to cite the full PBS interview of an accredited Duke University professor and archaeologist to give a clearer picture of how even respected scholars in the West try to weasel out of admitting the painful truth that there is no evidence to support the Exodus story. In service of this, I've decided to bold and italicize certain portions of the response to emphasize how this respected scholar, Carol Meyers, is attempting to equivocate on the value of truth. In particular, I'll be highlighting her fatuous attempt to declare that the lack of evidence for the Exodus tale requires a nebulous compromise between fact and fiction:

The source:
https://www.pbs.org/wgbh/nova/bible/meyers.html

MOSES AND THE EXODUS

Even people who know little about the Bible likely can recount the story of Moses leading the Israelites from Egypt in an extraordinary exodus. In this interview, Carol Meyers, an archeologist and professor of religion at Duke University, reflects on the significance of the Moses narrative in ancient times, the role it plays in American history, and why it continues to resonate with us today.

Editor's note: Carol Meyers, like other academic scholars, uses the term B.C.E. (Before the Common Era) instead of B.C. (Before Christ).

BEYOND FACT OR FICTION

Q: Questions about whether or not events in the Bible really happened evoke strong passions. As a biblical scholar, how do you see the issue of historical authenticity in terms of the earliest biblical accounts—the ones for which there is little archeological evidence?

Carol Meyers: *Too often in modern western thinking we see things in terms of black and white, history or fiction, with nothing in between.* But there are other ways of understanding how people have recorded events of their past. There's something called mnemohistory, or memory history, that I find particularly useful in thinking about biblical materials. It's not like the history that individuals may have of their own families, which tends to survive only a generation or two. Rather, it's a kind of collective cultural memory.

When a group of people experience things that are extremely important to their existence as a group, they often maintain collective memories of these events over generations. And these memories are probably augmented and elaborated and maybe even ritualized as a way of maintaining their relevance.

We can understand how mnemohistory works by looking at how it operates in more recent periods. We see this, for instance, in legends about figures in American history—George Washington is a wonderful example. Legends have something historic in them but yet are developed and expanded. I think that some of the accounts of the ancestors in the book of Genesis are similar. They are exciting, important, attention-grabbing, message-bearing narratives that are developed around characters who may have played an important role in the lives of the pre-Israelite ancestors.

Q: Let's turn to one of the most vivid figures in the Bible, Moses. Who is the Moses of the Bible, and could there have been such a person?

Meyers: *The Moses of the Bible is larger than life.* The Moses of the Bible is a diplomat negotiating with the pharaoh; he is a lawgiver bringing the Ten Commandments, the Covenant, down from Sinai. The Moses of the Bible is a military man leading the Israelites in battles. He's the one who organizes Israel's judiciary. He's also the prophet par excellence and a quasi-priestly figure involved in offering sacrifices and setting up the priestly complex, the tabernacle. There's virtually nothing in terms of national leadership that Moses doesn't do. And, of course, he's also a person, a family man.

Now, no one individual could possibly have done all that. So the tales are a kind of aggrandizement. He is also associated with miracles—the memorable story of being found in a basket in the Nile and being saved, miraculously, to grow up in the pharaoh's household. And he dies somewhere in the mountains of Moab. Only God knows where he's buried; God is said to have buried him. This is highly unusual and, again, accords him a special place.

"It's possible that a charismatic leader, a Moses, rallied people and urged them to make the difficult and traumatic and dangerous journey."

Q: What spurs the transformation of a real person into such a legendary figure?

Meyers: We can see the Moses narratives as the products of a period of trauma. We see this at other times and places. Think about our own American history. In the difficult period of the Revolutionary War, there's a lot of trauma and turmoil. Should people fight for freedom and risk losing everything? Or should they remain dominated by European colonial powers? And one man, George Washington, emerges as a superhero, the one in whom people could put their faith, who would take them to new terrain, who would lead them to independence. If you look at the biographies of George Washington that were written before 1855, you would think he was a demigod. The mythology about him is incredible.

In some ways, we have that kind of material about Moses. The hype about him is a way of expressing the fact that people could trust his judgment. They could trust that there would be success in this highly risky venture of leaving a place where they at least had food and water and going to a place where they might not have enough food and water. But they were apparently convinced it was worth the risk, if they might eventually be able to determine the course of their own lives and to escape the tyranny of Egyptian control.

EVIDENCE OF THE EXODUS

Q: You and other scholars point out that there isn't evidence outside the Bible, in historic documents and the archeological record, for a mass migration from Egypt involving hundreds of thousands of people. But it may be plausible that there was a much smaller exodus, an exodus of people originally from the land of Canaan who were returning to it. Is that right?

Meyers: Yes. *Despite all the ways in which the exodus narratives in the Bible seem to be non-historic*, something about the overall pattern can, in fact, be related to what we know from historical sources was going on at the end of the Late Bronze Age [circa 1200 B.C.E.], around when the Bible's chronology places the story of departure from Egypt.

Now, what is the evidence? First of all, during this period there likely were a lot of people from the land of Canaan, from regions of the eastern Mediterranean, in Egypt. Sometimes they were taken there as slaves. The local kings of the city-states in Canaan would offer slaves as tribute to the pharaohs in order to remain in their good graces. This is documented in the Amarna letters discovered in Egypt. So we know that there were people taken to Egypt as slaves.

There were also traders from the eastern Mediterranean who went to Egypt for commercial reasons. And there also probably were people from Canaan who went to Egypt during periods of extended drought and famine, as is reported in the Bible for Abraham and Sarah.

So Canaanites went to Egypt for a variety of reasons. They were generally assimilated—after a generation or two they became Egyptians. *There is almost no evidence that those people left.* But there are one or two Egyptian documents that record the flight of a handful of people who had been brought to Egypt for one reason or other and who didn't want to stay there.

Now, there is no direct evidence that such people were connected with the exodus narrative in the Bible. But in our western historical imagination, as we try to recreate the past, *it's certainly worth considering that some of them, somehow, for some reason that we can never understand*, maybe because life was so difficult for them in Egypt, thought that life would be greener than in the pastures that they had left.

And it's possible that a charismatic leader, a Moses, rallied a few of those people and urged them to make the difficult and traumatic and dangerous journey across the forbidding terrain of the Sinai Peninsula, back to what their collective memory maintained was a promised land.

ORIGINS OF THE ISRAELITES

Q: Do you think that these people returning to Canaan met up with other Canaanites in the hill country and became the people of Israel?

Meyers: *The emergence of ancient Israel in the highlands of Palestine is shrouded in clouds and mystery. We'll really never know the whole story. We can only conjecture how the inhabitants of new settlements in the highlands, in places where there never had been any settlements before, somehow began to identify with each other.* And, at least as I see it, they could have met with people who had made the trek across the Sinai Peninsula.

What was it that brought them together and gave them a new national identity, a new ethnicity? Many scholars, including me, would search in the theological realm. There is a belief in the Bible that the dream of escaping from Egypt and returning to an ancestral homeland could not have happened without supernatural intervention, divine intervention. And the group that had come from Egypt felt that one particular god, whom they called Yahweh, was responsible for this miracle of escape.

They spread the word to the highlanders, who themselves were migrants into the highlands, who perhaps had escaped from the tyranny of the Canaanite city-states or from an unsettled life as pastoralists across the Jordan River. And the idea of a god that represented freedom—freedom for people to keep the fruits of their own labor—this was a message that was so powerful that it brought people together and gave them a new kind of identity, which eventually became known by the term Israel.

REMEMBERING THE EXODUS

Q: So even though most of the early Israelites had not themselves made the exodus from Egypt, they adopt this story as part of their heritage.

Meyers: Yes. While very few Israelites may have actually made the trek across Sinai, it becomes the national story of all Israelites and is celebrated in all kinds of ways. Their agricultural festivals become celebrations of freedom, for instance. Many aspects of a new culture emerge and are linked with the "memories" of exodus.

The people who made the exodus from Egypt remember the experience, relive it, recreate it in rituals. They pass their rituals on to others, to future generations and to other people. We do this in our own American lives: Very few of us have ancestors who came over on the *Mayflower*, and yet that story has become part of our national story.

"The theme of the Exodus is an archetype in not only the Bible but in western culture in general."

Q: When was the story of the Exodus first written down?

Meyers: It's really hard to know when the story of the exodus first was put into written form. But it appears in one of the earliest poems in the

Bible, the Song of the Sea, found in the middle of the book of Exodus [Exod 15:1-22]. This victory hymn probably dates to the 12th century B.C.E.

It's also important to note that the Exodus is a theme that's mentioned over and over again in various parts of the Bible. And it's interesting to think about that in contrast, for example, to the early chapters in Genesis about the creation of the world and of Eve and Adam in the Garden of Eden. That motif rarely recurs in the Bible. It doesn't seem to be as important an aspect of biblical culture as was the exodus. The theme of a real people achieving freedom from oppression—that's something that resonates strongly with the biblical authors.

Q: And it's a theme that still resonates with us today.

Meyers: Absolutely. The theme of the exodus is an archetype in not only the Bible but in western culture in general. Even though it may be rooted in some cultural memory experienced by only a few people, it became a way of looking at the world that would have great power for generations and millennia to come—the idea that human beings should be free to determine the course of their own lives, to be able to work and enjoy the rewards of the work of their own hands and their own minds.

These are very powerful ideas that resonate in the human spirit. And Exodus gives *narrative reality* to those ideas. It would be compelling for peoples all over the world, wherever people find themselves subjected to domination and would like to live their lives in some other kind of way.

I think it's no accident that the founders of our own country, the United States, identified very strongly with the story of the Israelite exodus from Egypt. They felt that, in crossing the Atlantic Ocean and leaving the oppressive conditions of various European countries, they were coming to a place where they would be free from domination, where they would have religious freedom especially. And in the mythology of the colonial period in the United States, the crossing of the Atlantic somehow merged with the idea of the crossing of the Red Sea or Reed Sea of the Israelites. I think that the first seal of the United States actually depicted that kind of crossing.■

Interview conducted in August 2007 by Gary Glassman, producer, writer, and director of "The Bible's Buried Secrets," and edited by Susan K. Lewis, editor of NOVA Online[23]

To transpose and celebrate the mythic story of the Exodus onto the real life formation of the US has an assortment of unfortunate implications. Diseases that ravaged the Native Americans and actions of rape and torture imposed upon Native Americans by White settlers such as the Trail of Tears and US armed forces in the Chivington's Sand Creek Massacre abound in my mind. As I use to read and compare, I wondered if White settlers saw their slaughter of Native Americans as part of their duty to Jesus Christ and I wondered to what degree they thought the diseases that ravaged the Native Americans were a sign of their God, Jesus Christ, cursing innocent Natives for the crime of their existence. It was hard for me to read the accounts as it is clear that this is indeed how White settlers of the US viewed their genocide of the Native Americans. For the crime of being born another religious faith, they were subjected to cultural and physical genocide; rape and torture

---

[23] Meyers, Carol. "Moses and the Exodus." PBS, Public Broadcasting Service, 18 Nov. 2008, www.pbs.org/wgbh/nova/article/moses-exodus/.

abounded in Christian Boarding schools funded by the US government with the explicit effort to Christianize them as the nuns and priests raped innocent Native children. Just as casually as Carol Meyers skimmed over the death of first-born children of Egypt by the god Yahweh in the story of Moses, just as casually does she seem to omit the genocide of the Native Americans in the creation of the US. Invoking the Moses myth, a cultural "memory" based on fiction, could have helped to inspire and justify the genocide, gang rapes, and torture of Native Americans in the formation of the US. To so casually ignore such human rights crimes says it all to me on the morality of these Abrahamic myths. After all, if Moses had been a real person, then what would have been the moral difference between his actions and those of Islam's Prophet Mohammad? Would the difference just be in believing in the wrong version of the Abrahamic God? As shown from cited Biblical passages in the previous chapter, Moses endorsed the slaughter of young boys and the Old Testament endorsed the sexual exploitation of young girls. What good moral behavior is supposed to be gleaned from all this violence and hate in the Bible? What good comes from celebrating a country and ignoring how transposing these hateful myths requires the progeny of the new country to ignore a history of genocide on other peoples for the crime of simply existing? What about what was done to India under British rule or the Goa Inquisition? At the time of writing this, Great Britain is still legally a Constitutional Monarchy with no separation of Church and State; meaning that the actions of the British government, such as the four starvation campaigns upon India during colonial rule, were always interconnected with the Anglican religious faith. Are Indians, or really any human being with a conscience, suppose to believe that starvation campaigns are somehow policies that should be considered morally good? The next part is chiefly addressed to fellow Hindus, but I hope fellow Dharmic practitioners can use it as well. I understand some of this may be uncomfortable for some other denominations such as Sikhs, but please give it a full read.

It's with all of this in mind that I'd like to conclude by informing fellow Hindus of a different and perhaps more final path to peacefully ending the activities of Christian missionaries: *"I can say with all sincerity in my heart that I'd rather burn in hell as a Hindu than ever accept Christianity."* Christians are likely to view that in a smug way and believe that such sentiments are "childish" but I can't think of anything more nonsensical than a hateful religion that commits various forms of cultural genocide of anything that disagrees with it, physical genocide such as the Native Americans, and sexual exploitation of children (both Native Americans and more recently revealed to be cases across the world from the West to India) while proclaiming itself as the Chosen People despite all archaeological evidence disproving it. Archaeological evidence has thereby disproved the teachings and message of their so-called "Son of God" figure. Jesus Christ was nothing more than a narcissist with a God complex parading himself arrogantly as a God and declaring anyone who disagreed would be sent to hell. For me, a Hindu Atheist, the very concept of hell is absolutely laughable. If someone were to tell me they wish to give me the "good news" of Jesus Christ or I will burn in hell for all eternity, I will laugh in their face. To tell me I will burn in hell for disbelieving is the equivalent of telling me that a Flying Spaghetti Monster, Godzilla, a pink-polka dotted ethereal elephant, or a giant Pokemon will torture me in a magical theme park for all eternity for the crime of using my brain to reject certain ideas that I morally disagree with. Those examples of fictional characters are the intellectual equivalent of how I view concepts of hell and of heaven. I simply cannot view them with any degree of seriousness and if people sincerely believe them, then there is something mentally wrong with such people and they should be regarded as having some bizarre form of minor psychosis or some other form of mental illness because they seek to preach their mental health issues upon other people. To be clear, Christians hugging their beliefs in Christianity to themselves is fine, but if they begin preaching Christianity to others then I consider it to be a sign of mental health issues. They should seek help for their mental illnesses and stop annoying Hindus with their mental health issues since what they need is treatment for their suffering. Does that sound insulting? These people openly say they wish to test their faith by dying for it.

Why should such statements not be regarded as people of poor mental health using religion as an excuse to foist their psychotic delusions upon others?

Whether Christians are speaking in front of an entire village, knocking on your door, or screaming out in the streets; first, just imagine them with a white straitjacket behind a glass door as the scream about their love for Jesus Christ, then walk right up to them, put an arm calmly on their shoulder, look them right in the eyes with a smile, and say "I understand you have mental health issues and you believe in Jesus Christ because of them, please stop trying to convert us Hindus because it makes you feel good about your mental health problems." Be sure to carefully step away before they begin shouting louder about how they fully believe in Jesus Christ. Or, if you wish to keep it more brief, then try and say: "You have mental health issues because of your belief in Jesus Christ." and ideally you should hand them copies of some of the verses in the Bible that I shared in this book because most of these creepy and goofy people who shout about how Jesus Christ is God have never actually read the Bible.

Yes, that's right, these people shouting about Jesus Christ being their God have never actually read the Bible. I've always viewed them as empty and full of mental health issues that they're using the Bible as a coping mechanism for. I think, deep down, they know it is the truth about their lives too. They are empty of meaning and seek conversions so they don't have to think about how sad their lives are.

All that said, if you feel the same as I do, please just tell these Christian missionaries "*I'd rather go to hell for all eternity as a Hindu than accept Jesus Christ.*" Because it shows the following: First, we will not take their belief in hell seriously and we Hindus refuse to be bullied by it. *Second, this is probably the most effective and peaceful means of shutting down Christian conversions because they come to convert in order to justify their faith in Jesus Christ as their God, but instead you have introduced them to more doubt in their faith towards Jesus Christ.* They come and need to "see" people converting to make themselves feel better, but if you tell them that you don't take their beliefs seriously then they'll be forced to question their Christian faith. Third, it will do more to make them doubt their religious faith to see people say "I'd rather accept hell" than probably anything else that people say, because you show by example that the idea of hell is not real and it will not be taken seriously by you or others around you. Removing the religious intimidation, guilt, or bullying removes any coercive power that Christianity has over people. Nobody should care that some deluded, narcissistic rabbi from 100 AD Bronze age Palestine got himself killed for arguing with Roman soldiers or that he brainwashed people into worshipping him as a God. That is all the figure of Jesus Christ is; a myth based on a narcissist claiming godhood when he's done absolutely nothing for anyone since his death. It shouldn't have power over anyone in modern times. You may feel bad about doing this to someone of a different faith, but if Christian missionaries demand people convert, then show them why they are wrong by telling them that their beliefs are false and have no power over you as a Hindu, a Jain, a Sikh, or a Buddhist. Even if you believe in a hell, you don't believe in a Christian hell and you don't consider submission to Jesus Christ to be relevant in your life. If Christianity were real, I can say with full honesty and sincerity that I would rather burn in hell for all eternity than accept Christianity. I'd rather be tortured for an eternal afterlife for being a Hindu than accept Christianity. In other words, in my own personal moral compass: *I'd rather burn in hell for being who I am than go to a self-righteous heaven for who I am not.* I am not making some absurd joke when I say that I'd prefer to burn in hell as a Hindu and even as a Hindu Atheist than go to heaven submitting to some narcissistic, genocidal, child rapist absolving God known as Jesus Christ. I'd prefer to suffer in hell with my loving family, my loving friends, and the Native Americans who were wrongfully murdered by this man's hateful cult than spend all eternity praising Yahweh or Jesus Christ for all eternity. Eternal torture in hell, or even an absence of Yahweh in hell, would be a peaceful blessing compared to the eternal torture of heaven where I'd be compelled to praise a narcissistic lunatic for all eternity. If Christianity were real, I'd gleefully bear a curse for all eternity than submit to the hateful god, Yahweh or his narcissistic son, Jesus Christ; that is my truth as a Hindu.

Bibliography

1. "7 Steps to Grooming Your Young Christian Wife." *Biblical Gender Roles*, Wordpress, 29 July 2020, biblicalgenderroles.com/2020/07/16/7-steps-to-grooming-your-christian-wife/.

2. Alexander, Lori. "No Verses Command Husbands to Submit to Their Wives." *The Transformed Wife*, 9 Nov. 2020, thetransformedwife.com/no-verses-command-husbands-to-submit-to-their-wives/.

3. "Archeology of the Hebrew Bible." PBS, Public Broadcasting Service, 18 Nov. 2008, www.pbs.org/wgbh/nova/ancient/archeology-hebrew-bible.html.

4. Dutt, Barkha. "Opinion | In India, a Nun's #MeToo Moment Exposes the Failings of the Catholic Church." *The Washington Post*, WP Company, 1 Apr. 2019, www.washingtonpost.com/news/global-opinions/wp/2018/09/14/in-india-a-nuns-metoo-moment-exposes-the-failings-of-the-catholic-church/?utm_term=.6480250609be.

5. "How Many Angels Are There?" *GotQuestions.org*, 13 May 2019, www.gotquestions.org/how-many-angels-are-there.html.

6. *Ishtar's Descent into the Underworld (Page 1)*, www.inanna.virtualave.net/tammuz.html.

7. Licona, Mike. *Were People Raised When Jesus Died?* Youtube, 28 Apr. 2020, www.youtube.com/watch?v=rn50_pjn5Cg&feature=youtu.be.

8. Meyers, Carol. "Moses and the Exodus." PBS, Public Broadcasting Service, 18 Nov. 2008, www.pbs.org/wgbh/nova/article/moses-exodus/.

9. "National Liberation Front of Tripura." *Wikipedia*, Wikimedia Foundation, 9 Nov. 2020, en.wikipedia.org/wiki/National_Liberation_Front_of_Tripura.

10. "SOUTH ASIA | 'Church Backing Tripura Rebels'." *BBC News*, BBC, 18 Apr. 2000, news.bbc.co.uk/2/hi/world/south_asia/717775.stm.

11. "Static.reuters.com." Reuters, Reuters, static.reuters.com/resources/media/editorial/20150910/WilksDoctrinalPoints.pdf.

12. Sudhakaran, P. "Former Nun's Autobiography to Expose Catholic Church's Crisis in Kerala: Thiruvananthapuram News - Times of India." *The Times of India*, TOI, timesofindia.indiatimes.com/city/thiruvananthapuram/Former-Nuns-autobiography-to-expose-Catholic-Churchs-crisis-in-Kerala/articleshow/12476427.cms.

13. Tarico, Valerie. "Ancient Sumerian Origins of the Easter Story." *HuffPost*, HuffPost, 25 May 2011, www.huffpost.com/entry/ancient-mythic-origins-of_b_185455.

14. "Triple Deity." *Wikipedia*, Wikimedia Foundation, 29 Oct. 2020,

en.wikipedia.org/wiki/Triple_deity.
15. "What Happened to the Resurrected Saints Mentioned in Matthew 27: 52-53?" *United Church of God*, 9 Nov. 2010, www.ucg.org/bible-study-tools/bible-questions-and-answers/what-happened-to-the-resurrected-saints-mentioned-in.

About the Author

Jarin Jove is the pseudonym of Niraj Choudhary in his ill-conceived attempt at being clever by making a nickname based upon switching his first name and using the shortest name of his favorite planet in the solar system.

He has a personal blog: **www.jarinjove.com**. He can be reached via email at **jovejarin@hotmail.com** and on Twitter via the handle **@NocturneDream**. However, he prefers email correspondence.

He uses another pseudonym, Jason D. Visaria, to write fantasy novels and is the author of a dark humor book called *Ku Cuck Klan: The Family Values* written in order to exercise his Free Speech rights to mock Neo-Nazis and White Nationalists.

Copyright Notice: